Hobos to Street People:

Artists' Responses to Homelessness from the New Deal to the Present

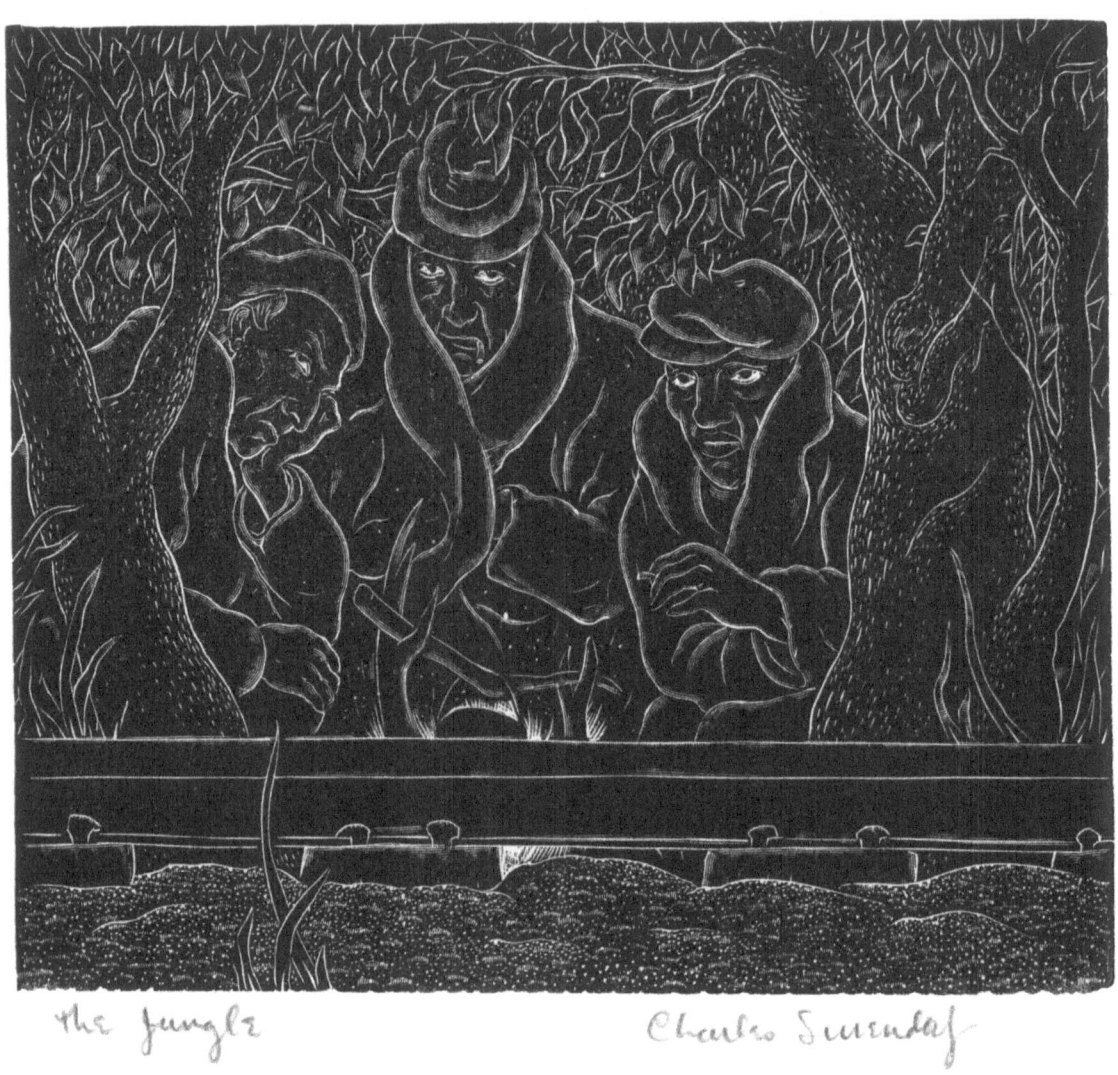

the jungle   Charles Surendorf

Charles Surendorf
(1906-1979)
The Jungle, c. 1940
Block Print, 5 x 6"
Courtesy of Surendorf Gallery Collection

Charles Surendorf worked for the San Francisco division of the WPA/FAP between 1937 and 1942, producing some 60 wood engravings and linoleum cuts. The jungle referred to in the title is the "hobo jungle," the name given to encampments along railroad tracks. Some of these jungles became famous as self-governing makeshift cities.

Hobos to Street People:
Artists' Responses to Homelessness from the New Deal to the Present

Art Hazelwood
With an afterword by Paul Boden

A traveling exhibition from

exhibit envoy

Curated by Art Hazelwood

Freedom Voices
2011

A traveling exhibition, 2009 to 2012, from Exhibit Envoy, funded by The James Irvine Foundation, LEF Foundation, and Fleishhacker Foundation.

Library of Congress Control Number: 2010942829
ISBN: 978-0915117-20-8

Freedom Voices
P.O. Box 423115
San Francisco, CA 94142
www.freedomvoices.org

Design: Jos Sances and Art Hazelwood
Editing : Marlene Griffith and Margot Pepper

Front cover:
Paul Weller
(1912- 2000)
Home, c. 1937
Lithograph, 10 1/2 x 14 1/2"
Reproduction Courtesy of Estate of Paul Weller
From the Collection of M. Lee Stone Fine Prints, Inc., San Jose, CA
Photo Credit: Robert Berger Photography

Back cover:
Christine Hanlon
(1954-)
Third Street Corridor, 1998
Oil on Canvas, 30 x 52"
Reproduction Courtesy of the Artist

Contents

Hobos to Street People:
Artists' Responses
to Homelessness from
the New Deal to the Present

By Art Hazelwood

Introduction

This book is based on a touring exhibition that first opened in February 2009—the time of the greatest economic downturn since the 1929 Stock Market Crash. It focuses on the work of artists who have sought to bring attention to poverty and homelessness, and it explores the various media that artists have used to get their message out. As the numbers of people living in poverty swells, it is a perfect time to look to the past for lessons and to reevaluate where we are today.

But even in these dark economic times, a strikingly consistent blindness dominates the discourse about poor and homeless people. The collective action and government support that followed the 1929 Stock Crash turns out to have been an anomaly. Government policies today mirror those of Poor Houses in the 19th century much more than they do those of the New Deal. A willful ignorance has again descended.

The image of homelessness planted in the mind of everyone living in America today is either a sad-faced man with a beard on a charity appeal or someone pushing a shopping cart overflowing with bags. But there is another image that still lingers in the collective memory. That image is of a migrant mother looking tired but proud, poor but noble, surrounded by her dirty-faced children. She looks into the camera lens, a camera wielded by Dorothea Lange, and she says to all who see her… "I am you."

In her time, during the Great Depression, America was a land in desperate straits. But the struggles of people to build a better society for themselves and their families created the ground upon which a more secure, more democratic, and more egalitarian society was built. It is a ground we have lived on for seventy-five years. That ground is crumbling under us. Again the poor are demonized by politicians and the press. Again economic insecurity is considered a sign, not of greed, but of a properly "flexible" workforce. Too often when people look into the migrant mother's eyes today, they do not see "I am you" but see only the "other," particularly if that migrant mother is from Latin America.

In the ideals of the New Deal programs of the 1930s there was a vision of a more inclusive society that valued everyone's humanity, and artists were a part of that vision. They were given jobs and enlisted to promote their image of society. The artists hired by the WPA were often poor and saw themselves reflected in the images they made and in the society they worked to help build.

Today, instead of being asked to contribute to building a better society with the WPA, an artist would more likely be sent to life skills training classes. The social goal of the WPA—of using art to lift humanity and address issues of poverty and homelessness—has disappeared. As society is increasingly becoming a commercial spectacle, mainstream imagery depicts homeless people as objects to be pitied or scorned and not as the human beings that they are. The role of the artist who creates work for social justice has shriveled.

And yet despite current campaigns to commercialize human values and emphasize corporate profits above community life, we are also seeing a reemergence of artists who reflect the hopes and struggles of an earlier generation. Like the artists of the 1930s, today's social activist artists like David Bacon, Jesus Barraza and Christine Hanlon, see themselves in the community. They give voice to the community and endeavor to make their art vehicles for social concerns—weapons against injustice.

The New Deal era's moral sphere that called for a "democratic culture" speaks to us through this book. Within these pages, you will witness a call to awareness and a call to action. The artists in this book have created works to chase away fear and ignorance and to silence scapegoating sound bites. They bring forward the nobility and the humanity of all people.

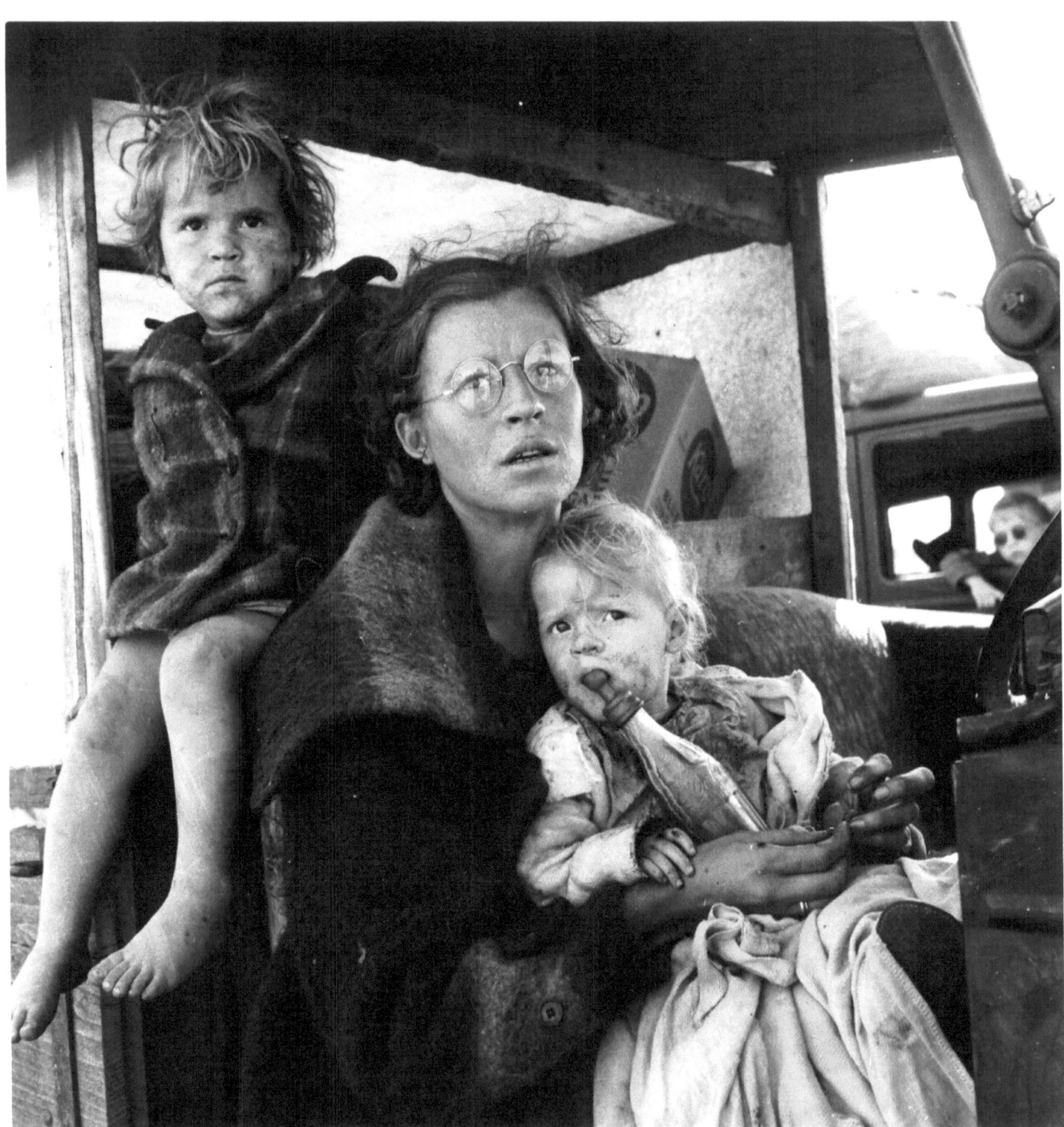

Hobos to Street People:
Artists' Responses to Homelessness from the New Deal to the Present

Two photographs of mothers and children surviving hard times together bridge the divide of seven decades between the Great Depression of the 1930s and contemporary homelessness. Dorothea Lange's image (figure #1) from 1939 and David Bacon's 2005 photo (figure #2) both call into question the morality of a society that creates such conditions. The Great Depression was not the first economic disaster for the country, but it was a terrible experience of displacement, loss, and uncertainty for millions. And for the first time in American history, the federal government, through the New Deal programs of Franklin Delano Roosevelt, stood up to address these concerns. Also for the first time, artists in large numbers stood up in addressing issues of social injustice including poverty. The Works Progress Administration Federal Arts Project (WPA/FAP) freed artists from the commercial art world to create art on issues of social importance. They unionized. They organized conferences and exhibitions. They made work for wide distribution on social issues and they contributed socially relevant art to various periodicals from the leftist *New Masses* to mainstream *Life*.

Yet, since the early 1980s, as a new wave of homelessness swept over the country, the federal government has largely washed its hands of the matter. In fact, the response has been to undo the policies that addressed poverty and homelessness from the Depression onward. This "Great Undoing" has proceeded at a steady pace to the present. And while there has been no government program since the end of the WPA that has liberated artists from the constraints of the commercial system, contemporary artists still managed to speak out. And they have continued to do so in increasing numbers. They have spoken out in alliance with activist groups as well as in periodicals, street posters and books. Much as Depression era artists, they have used any means at hand to disseminate their message. The artwork in this period was created to bear witness to social injustice, to make visible what is often hidden, to stand on the side of those who would be demonized for their poverty and to change the way society responds to poverty.

In comparing the two eras through the photographs by David Bacon and Dorothea Lange, many issues can be brought to light. Both photos present rural homelessness. Lange's image is of an American family displaced from the Dust Bowl of the Midwest. The family in the car is probably looking for agricultural work in the far north of California. The baby holds a coke bottle with a nipple on it. If they were like thousands of other migrants from the Dust Bowl, they were displaced by economic failure and environmental disaster.

Figure 1.
Dorothea Lange
(1895-1965)
Mother And Two Children On The Road Tulelake, Siskiyou County, California, 1939/1975
Library of Congress photograph on Agfa Portriga paper, 8 x 9 3/4"
Reproduction Courtesy of the Prints and Photographs Division, Library of Congress, Washington, D.C.
Collection of de Saisset Museum, Santa Clara University, NDA.6.686

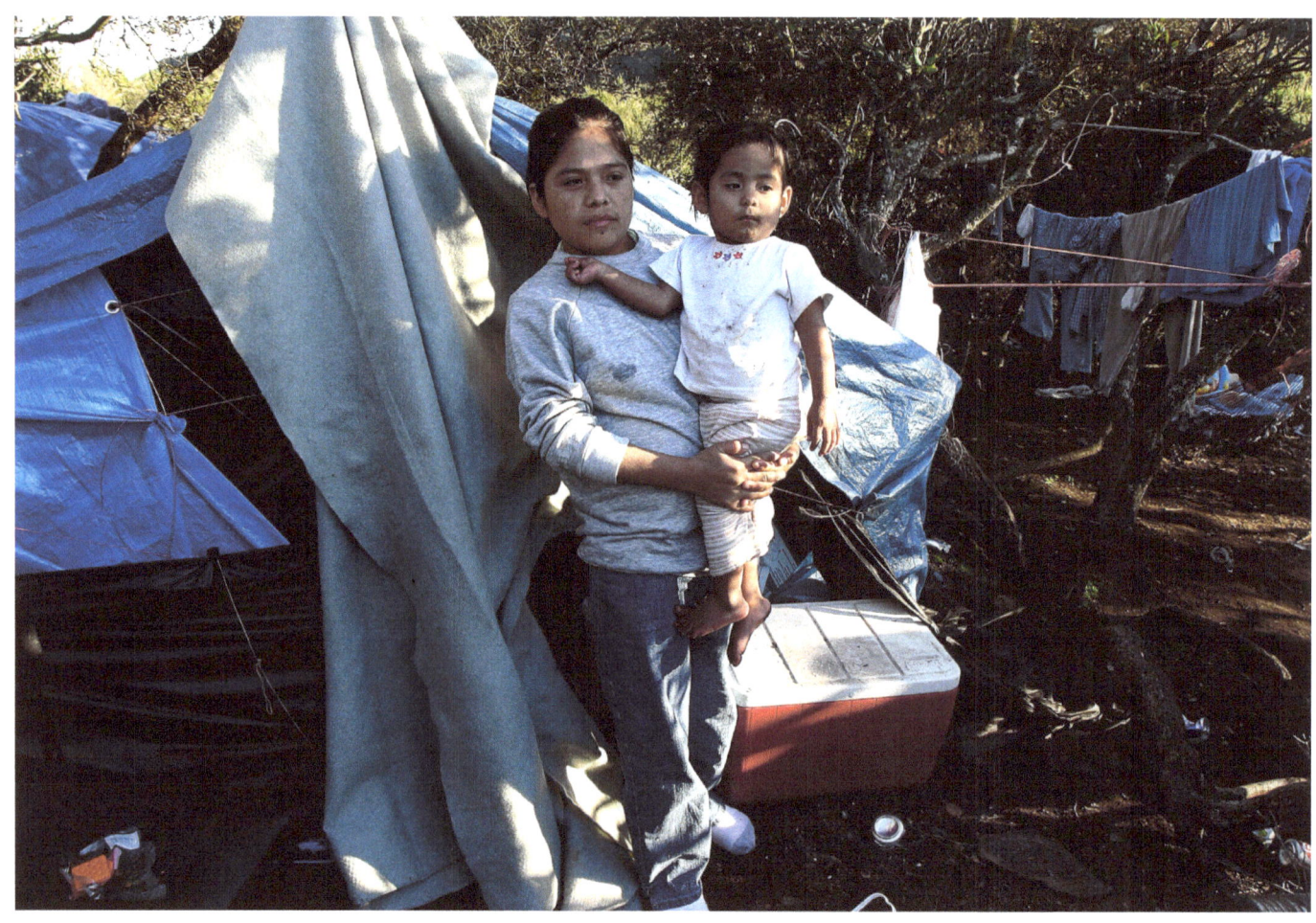

Figure 2.
David Bacon
(1948-)
*San Diego, Indigenous women and children are part of the community of farm
workers from Oaxaca, living in a camp on a hillside outside Delmar,* 2005
Photograph, 16 x 24"
Reproduction Courtesy of the Artist

David Bacon's photograph speaks to the global character of contemporary homelessness. Like the so-called Okies of the Depression, many of today's migrants have been displaced by environmental degradation and wider economic forces, such as the North American Free Trade Agreement (NAFTA[1]) which has led to the devastation of small farmers in Mexico. Both images show agricultural workers with inadequate housing, a car in one case, a tarp in another. Both images show that poverty and homelessness are not strictly an urban issue. And, perhaps most importantly, both images show the strength and nobility of their subjects. What is not depicted is the constant threat under which these women and their children live. Police intimidation and vigilante harassment, both then and now, keep these families perpetually on edge, unable to find a safe haven, always ushered onward to another nowhere.

The exhibition on which this book is based opened in San Francisco early in 2009, at the heart of the worst economic downturn since the Great Depression. As the concentration of wealth reached record highs, the banking system nearly collapsed, jeopardizing the world economy. Housing speculation, price manipulation and outright fraud led to a mortgage crisis that caused millions to lose their homes as unemployment skyrocketed. The media frantically called on homeless rights groups they'd ignored for years to help them find the newly homeless middle class family. They sought to uncover the "good homeless people," the ones deserving of

sympathy—a new Joad family, like the one from John Steinbeck's, *The Grapes of Wrath*.

At this same time of economic turmoil and during the course of the exhibition's nine month showing at the California Historical Society, museums in the San Francisco Bay Area were displaying fashion shows.[2] The majority of museums remained silent on the economy, or on any other social issue, for that matter. Perhaps there are valid reasons why the upper echelons of the art world were absorbed by haute fashion in a time of crisis, but it illustrates the general disconnect between art and society that has existed for a long time.

Yet for a brief time during the Great Depression, the art world turned broadly towards addressing issues of social importance. Leftist political activism paired with economic collapse and the decline of the commercial art market led to an increased social activism among artists. And the government turned to artists as well. It gave artists help in difficult times and, in turn, received a rich legacy of public art and powerful imagery about real life struggles, from housing, to lynching, to the fight against fascism. And during that time, the federal government also took it upon itself to address issues of poverty. It created the first federal program to address homelessness. It created programs for displaced farmers, for housing, for the security of families with children and for the elderly.

However, that moment passed. And while the legacy of FDR and the New Deal continues to exist in the form of buildings, bridges, hiking trails, post office murals, Social Security, the Security and Exchange Commission and many other government programs, its political strength has been undermined over time. When Ronald Reagan became president in 1980, he set for himself the goal of the destruction of the New Deal's social safety net, and the modern age of homelessness was born. Reagan redefined unemployment to make the numbers look less bleak,[3] but by 1983 emergency homeless shelters were opening all across the country.[4] And in the years since it has only gotten worse. The Clinton administration joined the fray in the 1990s by destroying the New Deal program Aid for Families with Dependent Children[5] and replacing it with temporary aid to needy families as part of his "Welfare Reform," and at the end of his second term Congress repealed the Glass-Steagall Act of 1933,[6] effectively removing the separation between Wall Street investment banks and depository banks. George W. Bush continued and accelerated the destruction of rural public housing and deregulated the economic sector until only a toothless, if not sycophantic, bureaucracy remained. The onslaught of the mortgage meltdown is just one result of this long line of erosion. Long ago, the art world resumed its games of one-upmanship, of art stars, and fashion shows.

When the media went searching for the new Joad family in 2009, they weren't interested in understanding or explaining the real origins of homelessness. They were only interested in previously secure homeowners losing their homes. In reality, homelessness has hit local communities like a tidal wave: destruction of public housing, loss of job security, veterans returning from wars physically and psychologically damaged, urban redevelopment, declining real wages, the emergence of a credit-driven economy, and the mass deinstitutionalization of people with mental illness all have contributed. For the past three decades, however, rather than reporting on these real causes, nearly every mainstream media story on homelessness has been sprinkled with references to urine, feces, and hypodermic needles. The media has systematically failed to report on the greatest shift of wealth from the poor and middle class to the rich in U.S. history.

The Depression, triggered by the Stock Market Crash of 1929, was followed by bank runs, nationwide unemployment, farm foreclosures and severe drought coupled with soil erosion that led to the Dust Bowl in the Midwest. The cities and the countryside were full of poor people. In 1931, 1,200 to 1,500 economic migrants arrived in California from the Midwest every day[7]. Unemployment in 1929 stood at 3% and by 1933, 25% of all workers were unemployed.[8] By 1933 over a million and a half Americans were homeless, out of a population of 125 million or 1.2%.[9]

And here we are again. In 2009, the US Department of Education reported that nearly 1 million children in public schools were homeless. As many as 3.5 million people were homeless nationwide from a population of 310 million, or 1.13%—close to the same percentage of homeless people as in 1933. In 2010 the number of Americans living in poverty rose to one in six, or 47.8 million, up from one in seven in 2009.[10] We saw a 9 to 12% increase of people in shelters.[11] Unemployment was above 10% nationwide, although the real unemployment figure was closer to 16% and in some counties in California the unemployment figures rivaled those of the Depression.[12] Veterans of the Iraq and Afghan wars were moving into homelessness at faster rates than ever before, according to the Veterans Administration.[13] And, of course, foreclosures were up everywhere in the country: 3.4 million families experienced foreclosure in 2009.[14]

The federal government's response, however, has been drastically different than during the Depression. Instead of creating programs and support, the George W. Bush administration in its last four years cut all forms of spending on low income housing by over two billion dollars, while increasing spending on homeless assistance by only 157 million dollars.[15] This pattern of cutting spending on housing while minimally increasing homeless assistance speaks to a belief that poverty isn't a system wide failure but simply a failure of individuals, and that the way to address poverty is to

fix broken people. Since the 1980s, the sights of the federal government have turned from fighting poverty to handing out blankets.

No longer does the government see its role as addressing the problems of inadequate housing, or of preventing childhood homelessness, or even in addressing the needs of returning veterans. Legislation in 1998 to amend the New Deal era Housing Act removed the original goal of "a decent home and a suitable living environment" and scaled back federal responsibility for decent living conditions. Now the role of government is simply charity as a mask to hide inaction. But the charity given is "means tested" and only selectively offered to those that fit the newest, ever changing, government definition of need.

Barack Obama's administration has implemented some programs to address the mortgage crisis, such as requiring states to provide at least 90 days to tenants to find housing after foreclosure. In some states, tenants were previously given as few as three days. The 2009 Recovery and Reinvestment Act also included money for homelessness prevention and there has been some movement towards funding low-income housing.[16] But this hardly represents a turning point in national priorities.

During the Depression there was a different idea. The New Deal created job programs, it addressed the dislocation of farmers from the Midwest and it created agencies to build housing—laying the groundwork for a comprehensive federal response to poverty and homelessness.

And artists responded too. The artists of the Great Depression era were brought together by economic need and the funding provided by government programs, as well as by their radical political ideology. They saw the artist's role in society to be one of active engagement and took steps to address social injustice. This belief in the social value of art was almost immediately attacked by the establishment art world in the post-war era. Many artists were threatened and their political beliefs driven underground by Cold War anti-communist witch hunts spearheaded by Senator Joseph McCarthy.

But eventually another generation of artists reemerged that began to address social issues. By the mid-1980s, American cities again became crowded with bread lines and panhandlers, and artists again began to respond. These later-day artists had no government support and most had no unifying political perspective. In many cases they didn't share the economic distress of their subjects either. But they joined together with activists, and found ways to reconnect to a tradition of political art that had largely been suppressed under McCarthyism.

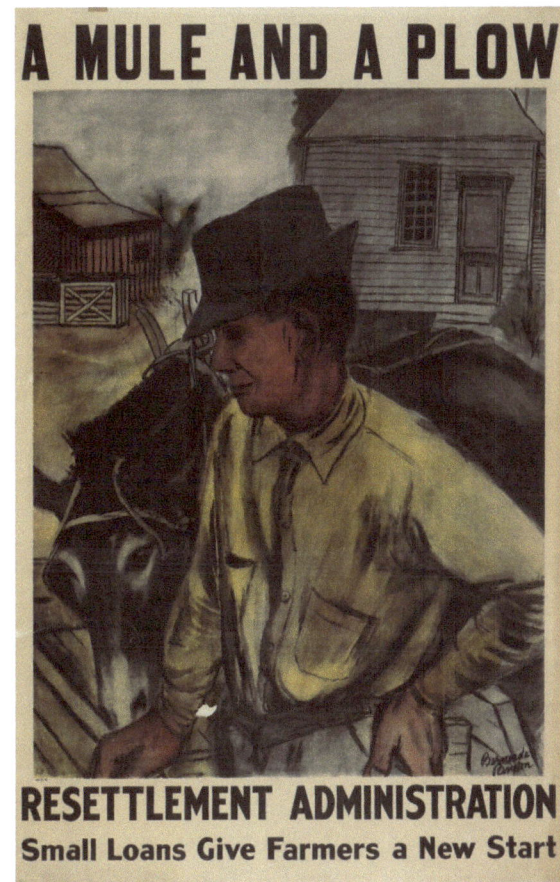

Figure 3.
Bernarda Bryson Shahn
(1903 – 2004)
A Mule and a Plow,
1935 – 1937, lithograph on paper, 43 x 30"
Courtesy of the Prints and Photographs Division,
Library of Congress, Washington, D.C.

Homelessness in the Depression

While homelessness has always been a part of the "American" story, it has gone though distinctive phases. The regular boom and bust cycles of the 19th century, the Industrial Revolution, the Civil War and Reconstruction, and the ever-spreading reach of the rails throughout the country – they all shaped the characteristics of homelessness in its multiple incarnations and appellations: bums, tramps, vagrants, hobos, transients, street people.

Reactions to homelessness have varied also: from the 19th century's fear of armed bands of hobos riding into town on the rails to the nostalgic "Little Tramp" of Charlie Chaplin. On balance, the reactions to homeless people has been punitive: laws against vagrancy; work houses that required chopping wood or other labor in exchange for food and in order to build up the "work ethic;" laws against people moving into town without visible means of support. All operated on the principle that homeless people are dangerous and lazy and need to be reformed and taught the value of work. It stands to reason that every economic downturn produces more poor people in need. But like clockwork, again and again, the reaction has been to criminalize poverty. Its modern guise can be seen in the Welfare Reform of the 1990s, the Welfare to Work programs which require community service and street sweeping, and a myriad of "Quality of Life" crimes in cities nationwide: laws against sleeping, street-vending, panhandling, obstruction, intent to lodge, and even sitting.

In light of this, the response to the devastation wrought on the nation by the economic collapse of the Great Depression stands out as something of a miracle, in contrast to both earlier and later responses.

Government Responses during the Depression

In 1932, as the economic effects of the Depression were starting to bite, an army of nearly 20,000 World War I veterans and their families, more than 40,000 in all, marched on Washington DC demanding to be paid the benefits promised them at the end of the war. They camped out for more than a month on the Anacostia Flats across the river from DC. They were known as the Bonus Marchers and were one of a long line of protest movements by poor people.

President Herbert Hoover put General Douglas MacArthur in charge of removing the marchers. MacArthur, later claiming to fear a communist revolution, gave the order for what became the last cavalry charge in US military history, ironically against US veterans. The Bonus Marchers were routed with fixed bayonet and gas, their tents were burned, an unknown number were killed. For many Americans, this action was another failure by Hoover to face up to the enormity of the challenge of the Depression. By this time, many unemployed families lived in Hoovervilles, informal shanty-towns named with conscious irony after the president who had promised Americans a "permanent plateau of prosperity." Hoover was shortly thereafter defeated and Franklin Delano Roosevelt became president.[17]

Roosevelt's New Deal represented a major shift in American policy. With the background of the Bonus Marchers, widespread strikes and increasing political action by the unemployed, unions and tenants, the Federal Government, for the first time directly addressed issues of poverty.[18] Among the new agencies created in the first 100 days of FDR's presidency was the Federal Transient Services (FTS) that established transient service centers in cities and rural areas throughout the country. It made federal grants available to local communities to open shelters, operate food kitchens, and extend other services to homeless people. Several innovative programs opened around the country, some including educational programs, and libraries. At its height, the FTS was serving close to half a million people. But the agency never had strong political support and was phased out in late 1935. It was assumed that other New Deal work programs like the WPA and Civilian Conservation Corps would take over in providing the support needed for those served by the FTS.[19]

Other New Deal programs did address different aspects of poverty. Aid to Families with Dependent Children (AFDC), commonly known as Welfare, addressed poverty in children by providing financial aid through the states for children whose parents were disabled, absent, deceased or unemployed. The Social Security act of 1935 established an old-age pension to reduce the suffering of older Americans.[20] Rural poverty programs sought to build up infrastructure and resettle farmers onto more productive land or help them with loans to be able to stay on their land (figure #3). The Farm Security Administration and its predecessor, the Resettlement Administration, operated ninety-five farm labor camps that gave migrants clean water and safety and stood in bright contrast to the Hoovervilles. Unfortunately, the 75,000 people who used these camps were a small fraction of the 2.5 million displaced out of the Dust Bowl states of the Midwest.[21]

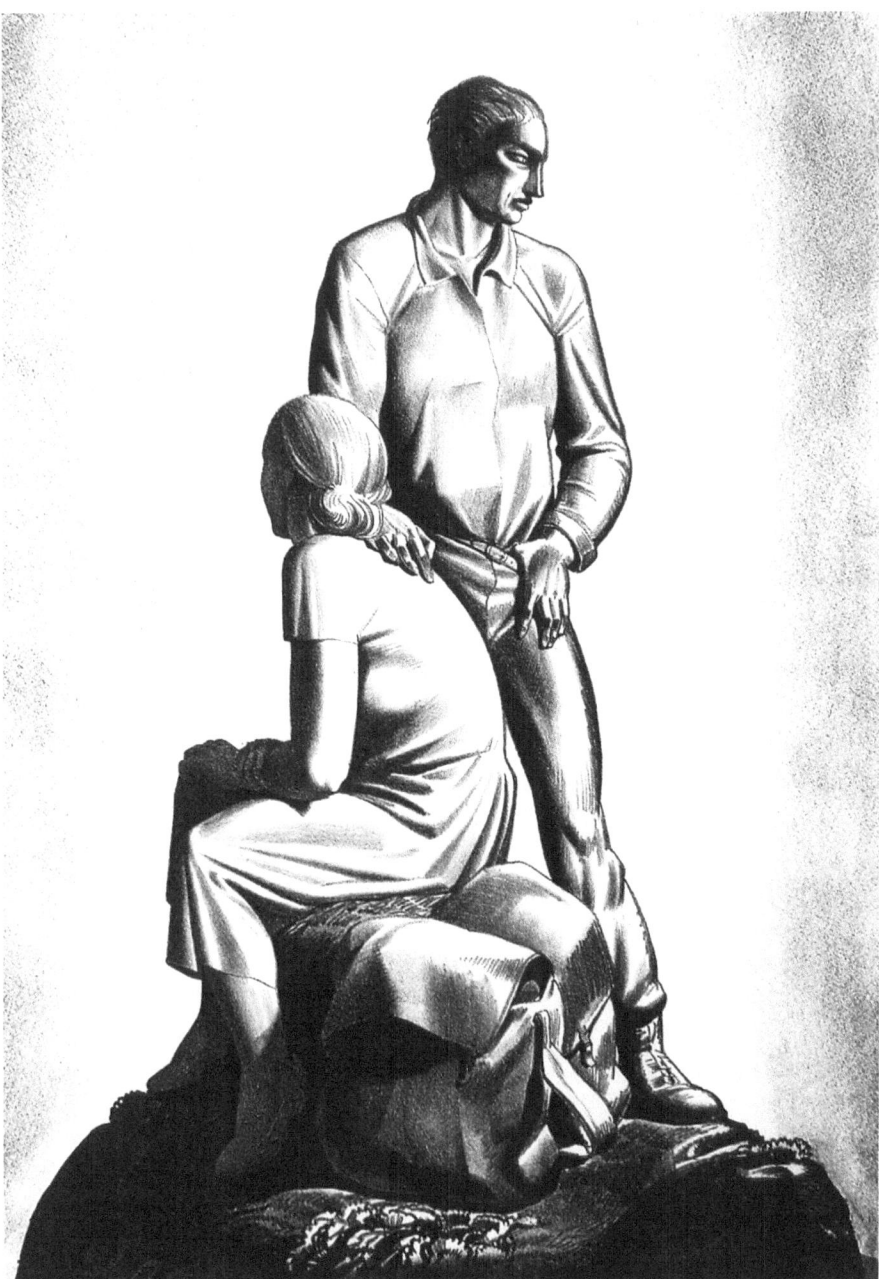

Figure 4.
Rockwell Kent
(1882-1971)
And Now Where? 1936
Lithograph, 13 x 9 3/8″
Reproduction Courtesy Plattsburgh State Art Museum, State University of New York, SUNY, Rockwell Kent Gallery and Collection. Bequest of Sally Kent Gorton

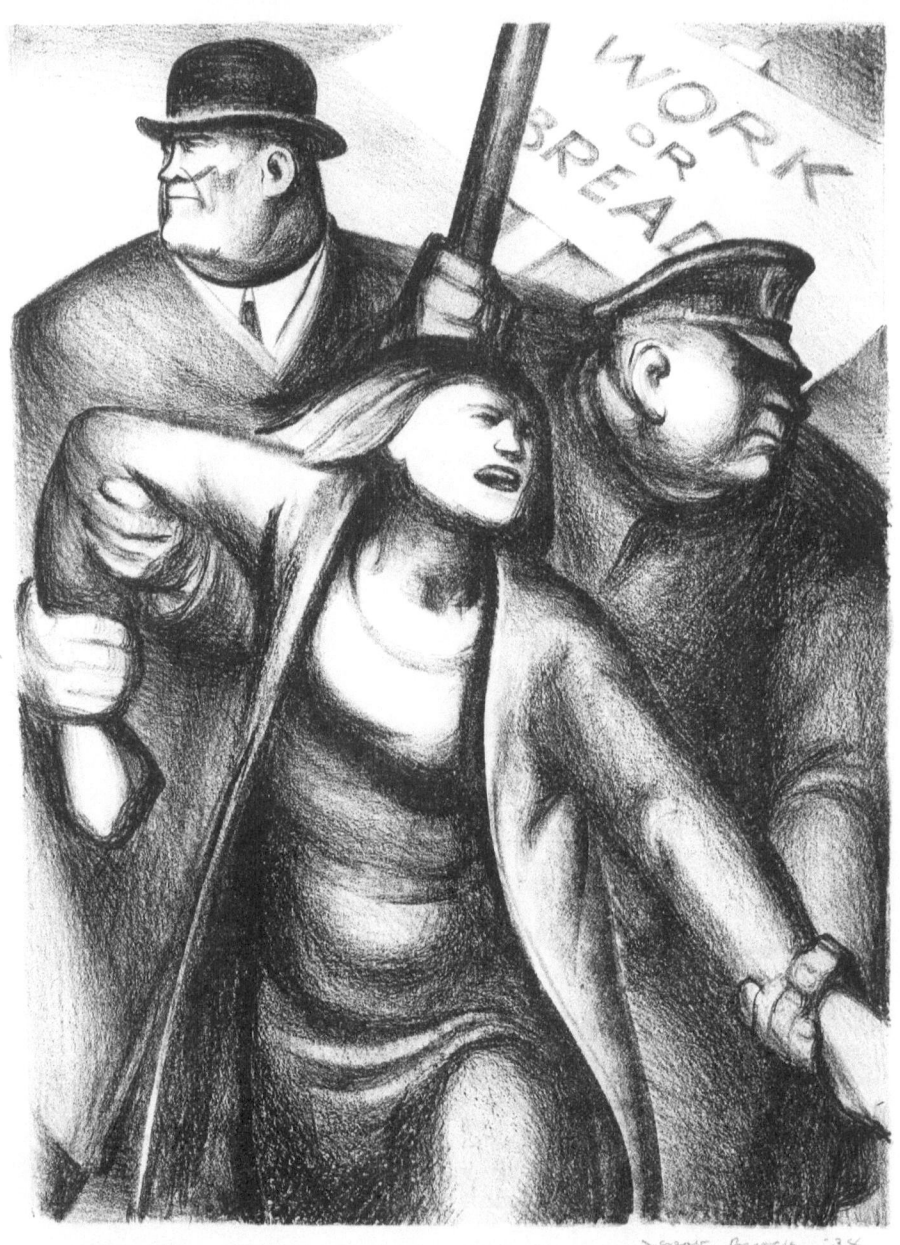

Figure 5.
Jacob Burck
(1907-1982)
The Lord Provides, 1934
Lithograph, 12 x 9 1/16"
Reproduction Courtesy of
Conrad and Joseph Burck
Collection of M. Lee Stone Fine
Prints, San Jose, CA
Photo Credit:
Robert Berger Photography

Art and Engagement

There were several forces that changed the face of art in the Depression but among them, the very real economic collapse weighed most heavily. The sudden and massive collapse of the economic order had jolted artists. Many had been employed in the commercial art and illustration business, but most were marginally employed at best before the Depression. Now their situation became much worse. Rather than turn against each other and fight over the shrinking pie, several factors encouraged a more communal response. Marxism and its principles of more equitable distribution was much more openly avowed than at any time since. It provided a framework to understand the economics of the times and offered a solution through worker solidarity. Whether or not artists were Marxist, they believed in a communal answer to the situation of the moment.[22]

The impact of the art and ideas of the Mexican muralists, especially Diego Rivera, had its influence as well. The example of Mexican artists creating work that sought to educate and praise the poor in Mexico inspired a generation of American artists to think of art as being in the service of the community.

Then of course, there was the added threat of fascism both at home and abroad. Hitler came to power in Germany in 1933. The Spanish Civil War broke out in 1936 and the call to support the anti-fascist Popular Front Government forces in Spain inspired many artists to work to raise funds, to participate in exhibitions that drew attention to the struggle, and in some cases (including printmaker, Mildred Rackley and painter Irving Norman), to travel to Spain to assist the war effort.

Increasingly, artists began to realize their interests lay with the working class. They began to reinterpret their roles as artists, sought to build solidarity with working people, to explicitly criticize capitalism, and to make art available to all people. In the 1930s, all this was new and powerfully-felt and most importantly, put into practice.

The art programs of the WPA dovetailed nicely with many of these beliefs. Beginning in 1933 the Public Works of Art Project (PWAP) was followed by the 1935 Federal Art Project (FAP) under the Works Progress Administration (WPA). The WPA was the largest employer in the country until well into World War II. Within the FAP were divisions for graphics, posters, easel painting, sculpture, as well as a division to create murals for government buildings. The FAP employed more than 5,000 visual artists. The Graphic Arts Division of the FAP alone employed over 800 artists spread throughout 36 cities. These artists were required to produce artwork at regular intervals for which they were paid about $24.00 a week.[23]

Those who were hired by the WPA/FAP shared their allegiance with both workers and poor people. In order to be hired, artists had to demonstrate that they were both artists and destitute.[24] Through the WPA artists became workers, and their camaraderie with each other—freed from the competitive gallery marketplace—not only allowed them to focus on issues they saw as important, but also intensified their sense of solidarity with other workers.

Artists were also employed by the Treasury Department Section of Fine Arts. This department was established in 1934 and was responsible for many of the murals painted in public buildings during the Depression. In addition, the Resettlement Administration (later the Farm Security Administration, FSA) had a photographic division which employed photographers to document the plight of farmers as well as its own work.

The FSA Information Division's Historical Section was headed by Roy Stryker who, on his own initiative, hired photographers who created one of the greatest collections of photographs ever assembled in the United States, numbering 270,000. Dorothea Lange was one of 22 photographers employed by the FSA. She took some of the best-known photographs of the era and for many people her work still defines the Depression. But many other significant photographers worked for the FSA, including Walker Evans, Ben Shahn, and Gordon Parks.[25]

Stryker encouraged the photographers to portray the humanity of their subjects. It was a sentiment widely shared at the time. Holger Cahill, who was the overall head of the Federal Arts Project of the WPA, expressed similar interests in creating artwork that spoke to people's humanity. People like Stryker and Cahill who led these organizations were remarkable in their passionate promotion of the humane purpose of artwork, but their ideals were not uncommon. They mirrored those of many artists at the time, even those not employed by the government.

Rockwell Kent (figure #4) was among the most successful printmakers during the Depression. His work was sometimes published in large inexpensive editions, as well as in book illustrations and posters. He was a prominent figure at conferences and in leftist artist organizations. His sentiment was clearly in line with Cahill and Stryker.

The Depression was the first time in US history that such a widespread movement of artists began to address issues of human rights. They actively found ways to influence society through exhibition and distribution of their work. The large number of poor, displaced and homeless people was only one important focus. Artists organized exhibitions on other social and political themes such as anti-lynching and anti-fascist. They organized conferences. They unionized and struggled for better conditions for artists in relation to the WPA and the wider art world. They sought to protect foreign-born artists from being excluded from WPA programs. They contributed to publications and they made posters.

An important voice for social commentary in the visual arts was the *New Masses* magazine. From 1926 to 1948, *New Masses* integrated politics, literature and art with a Marxist perspective. The magazine reached a circulation of 25,000 in 1935 and was a vehicle for many artists of the left, including Jacob Burck (figure #5), Richard V. Correll (figure #11), Hugo Gellert, Reginald Marsh, and Rafael Soyer.[26]

Many artists of the time joined and organized for political objectives and in 1936 the American Artists' Congress was formed as part of the Popular Front of a united Left against fascism. The Artists' Congress represented the most active moment of their political involvement. Hundreds of artists joined the group at the beginning and hundreds more came to the conventions. They organized exhibitions, including the important show, *Against War and Fascism*. They raised money for the Abraham Lincoln Brigade fighting the Fascists in Spain and they were responsible for bringing Picasso's painting of *Guernica* to New York. They pressed the US Congress to establish a permanent Bureau of Fine Arts. They also published *Art Front* magazine, which represented the artistic side of the Popular Front against fascism.[27]

Many other artist groups were formed in the 1930s. Influenced by a long tradition in printmaking, several of these groups promoted the ideal of printmaking as a democratic art form. Associated American Artists began in 1934 with the idea of selling prints at low prices: $5 each. They produced hundreds of editions by some of the most well-known artists of the day, including Thomas Hart Benton and Grant Wood.[28] The hope of reaching a more populist audience through large editions of prints inspired many artists to create work in this media. The preferred techniques were lithography and wood engraving. Both could be printed more quickly and inexpensively than the previously more widespread technique of etching.

Rockwell Kent produced *And Now Where?*, (figure #4) for American Artists Group in an unsigned edition of 1000. Jacob Burck's lithograph *The Lord Provides* (figure #5) was created for a portfolio of prints by the Contemporary Print Group in 1934. This portfolio of inexpensive prints included works by Jose Clemente Orozco, George Grosz and others.

Artist-Worker Alliances

The momentum toward artist worker alliances continued after the Depression. One model for artists and activists to work together in a politically-engaged environment was the California Labor School in San Francisco. A communist union school that included courses for union organizing, trade skills, and culture, it was accredited for college level work and was active from 1942 to 1957. It was shut down as a result of the anti-communist atmosphere of the Cold War. The Graphic Arts Workshop print studio, spun off from the Labor School, survives to this day as its only vestige.[29]

Before it was shut down, the Labor School art department attracted a wide range of local and international artists with a strong connection to Mexico and the populist art traditions there. Pablo O'Higgins, an American who lived in Mexico and co-founded the collective printmaking workshop *Taller de Gráfica Popular* (T.G.P) in Mexico City, briefly taught at the Labor School. The art department of the Labor School was inspired by the T.G.P.[30]

Russian-born artists Victor Arnautoff and Anton Refregier (figure #35) also taught at the Labor School. For a time, Italian-born Giacomo Patri was the head of the art department. Before joining the Labor School, Patri worked as a newspaper illustrator, the same trade as the main character in his 1938 book of linoleum cut prints, *White Collar* (figure #6). In this novel without words, Patri tells a story of the increased political radicalization of the central character. The novel reflected the economic despair that white collar workers shared with blue collar workers during the Depression. At the beginning he dreams

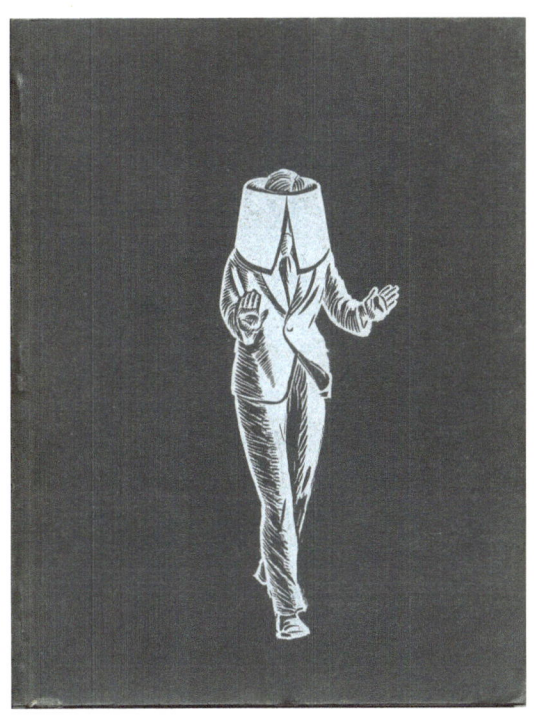

Figure 6.
Giacomo Giuseppe Patri
(1898-1978)
White Collar, 1940, 1st Edition Book Printed from Original Linocut Blocks, 10 3/4 x 8 1/4"
Reproduction Courtesy of Georges Rey From the Collection of M. Lee Stone Fine Prints, San Jose, CA

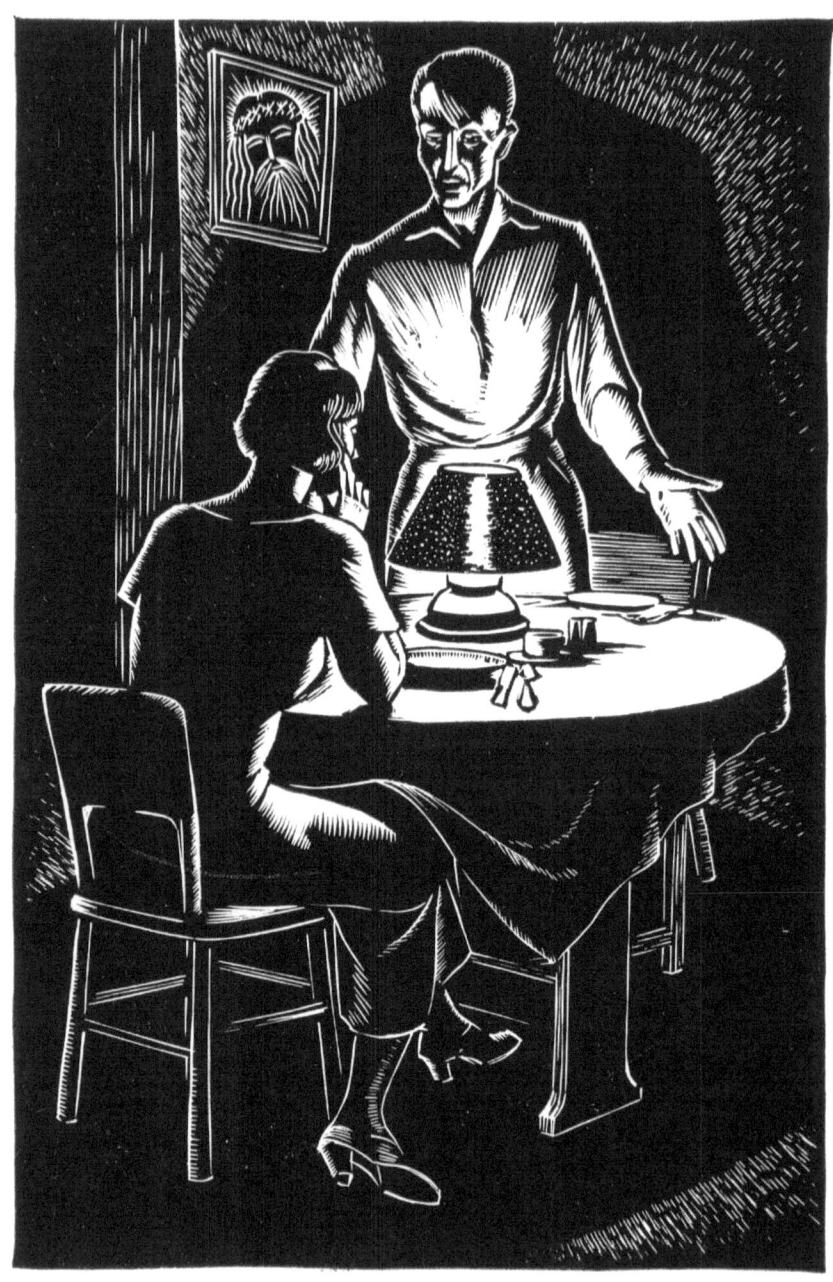

of the road to success but his hopes are repeatedly dashed along the way. As the economic forces of the Depression pull him and his family down, he begins to see that he is part of a wider community of disenfranchised workers. The series of events, the stock crash, job loss, health problems, foreclosure, is a litany of the insecurities faced during the Depression. The family moves from home to apartment to shelter until they finally are forced to move into a tent city. His belief in capitalism shattered; he envisions himself joining an army of the dispossessed marching in revolution.

Figure #7 depicts the shock after the Stock Market Crash of 1929. Figure #8 shows a visit to the doctor for an abortion. The following frame in Patri's book shows what is written in the book the doctor shows them, "Abortion, A Felony". As the bills add up, the family pawns their belongings (figure #9).

Another artist organization based in New York and called An American Group presented *Roofs for 40 million: an Exhibition on Housing* at Rockefeller Center in 1938.[31] The show was created in response to FDR's second inaugural address.

> *I see one-third of a nation ill-housed, ill-clad, ill-nourished. It is not in despair that I paint you that picture. I paint it for you in hope—because the Nation, seeing and understanding the injustice in it, proposes to paint it out.*
> Franklin D. Roosevelt
> 1/20/1937

This address also inspired a play. *One-Third of a Nation*, by Arthur Arent, was created by the WPA Federal Theatre Project and presented at theaters around the country (figure #10). Citing footnoted data and employing a cinematic style, the play explores causes behind the decrepit and overpriced housing of major urban centers. Screenprints produced by the WPA/FAP Poster Division were created for showings of *One-Third of a Nation* in many cities, including New York, Philadelphia and Portland, Oregon.

The Poster Division's screenprints were primarily made as event announcements. In the WPA/FAP several artists experimented with artistic applications of screenprint to develop it from a commercial media into an artistic one. Its ease of production and speed of printing makes it the favored political art technique today.

This proliferation of groups, publications and activities among artists represented a tremendous amount of organization on a broad range of social and political themes. In addition to poverty and homelessness, the most organized work by artists focused on anti-fascist and anti-lynching campaigns as well as significant support for improved conditions for coal miners. This politicization of artists on a broad range of issues and the clarity with which they saw the interconnectedness of all these issue was the product of an atmosphere of artistic ferment that may have been supercharged by the WPA/FAP but was then widely developed by artists' efforts to organize.

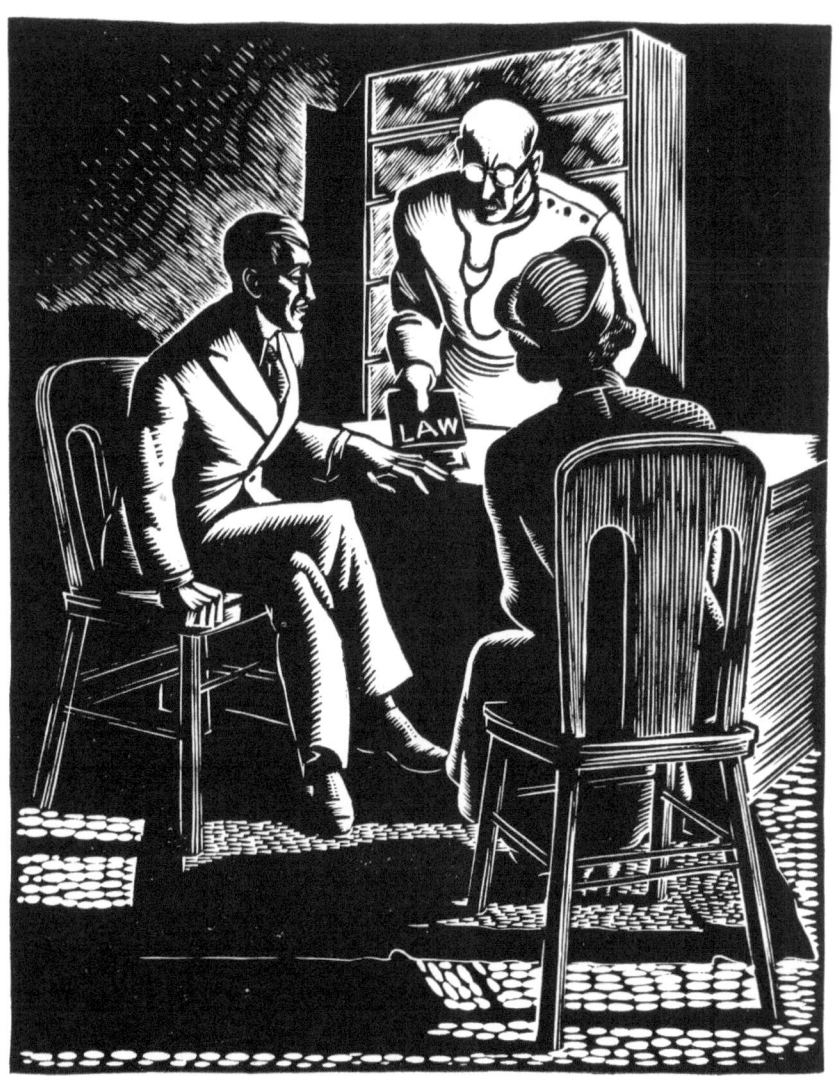

Figure 7, 8.
Giacomo Giuseppe Patri,
(1898-1978)
Linocut Print Page from the Book,
White Collar, 1938, 6 1/2 x 4 1/4" (facing) 6 1/8 x 5" (this page)
Reproduction Courtesy of Georges Rey
Photo Credit: Robert Berger Photography

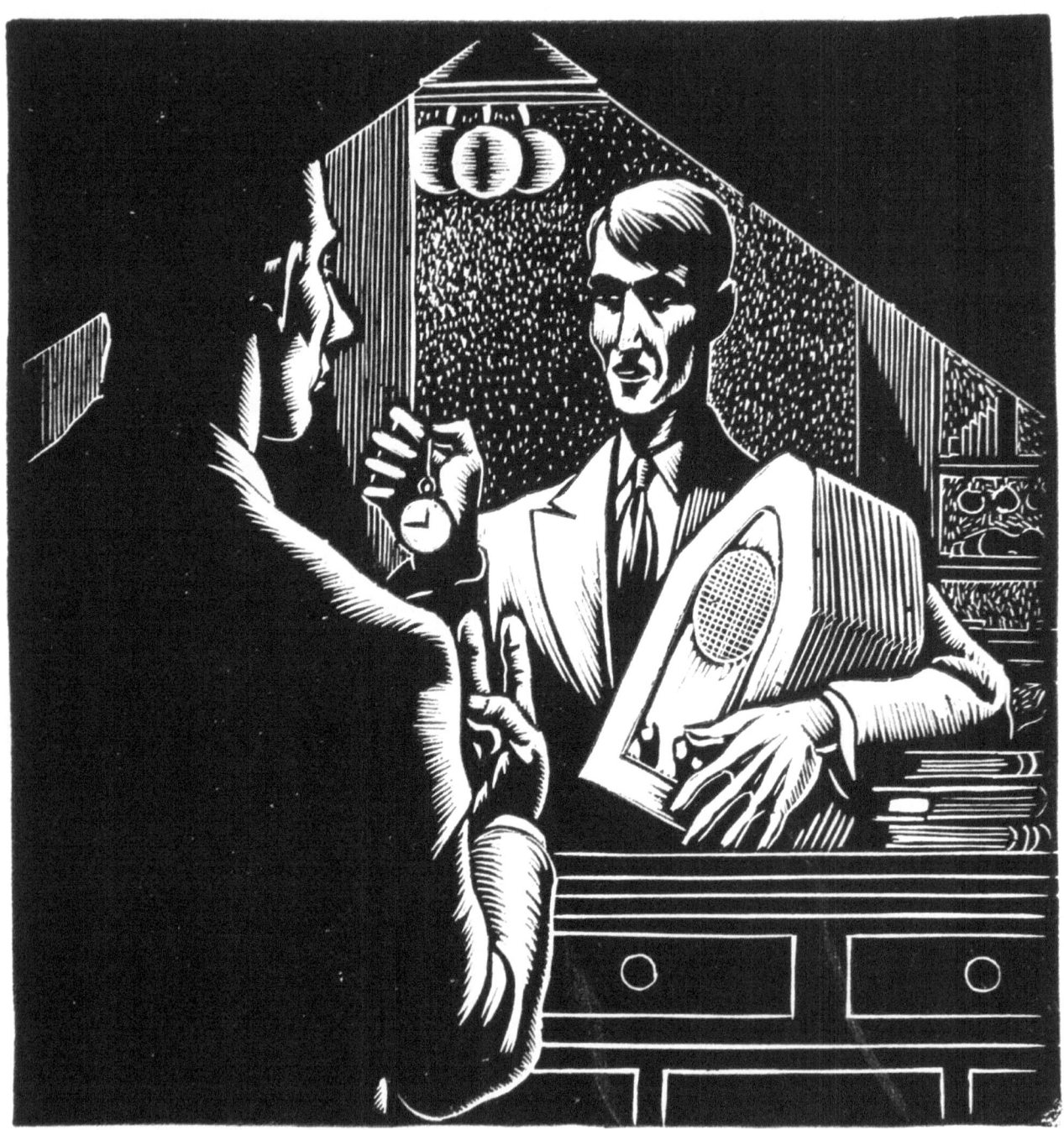

Figure 9.
Giacomo Giuseppe Patri
(1898-1978)
Linocut Print Pages from the Book,
White Collar, 1938, 4 x 3 3/4"
Reproduction Courtesy of Georges Rey
Photo Credit: Robert Berger Photography

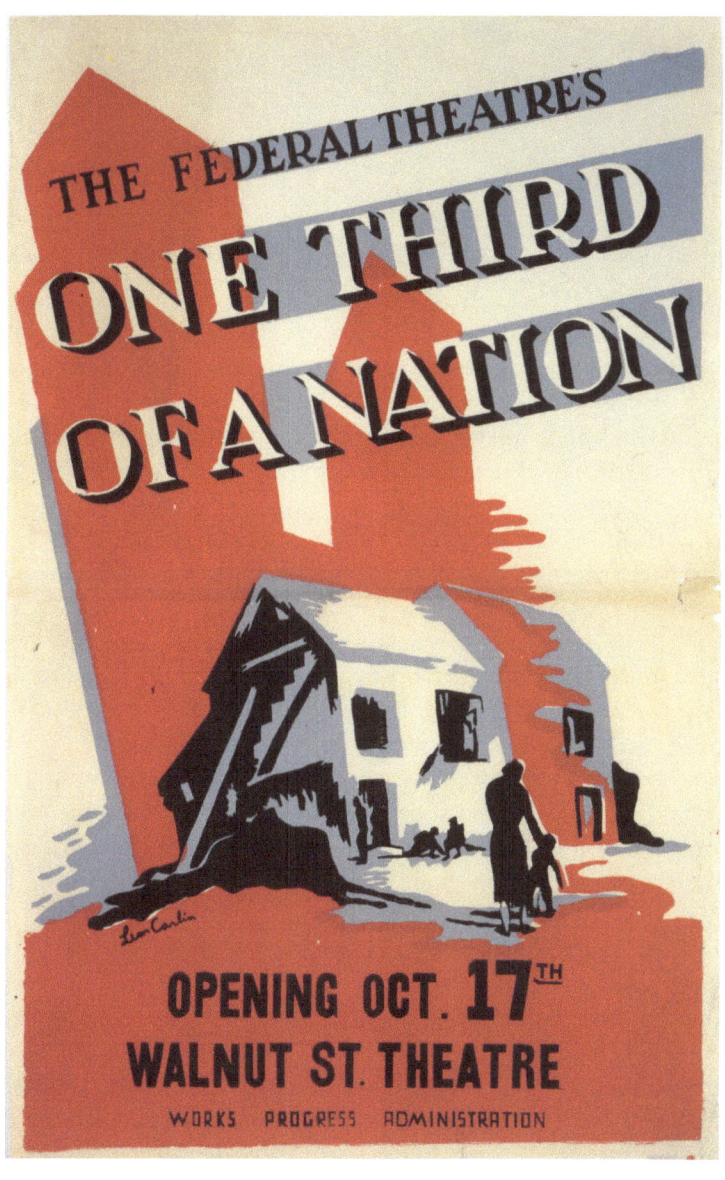

Figure 10.
Leon Carlin
(dates unknown)
One Third of a Nation, 1938
Screenprint poster for Federal Theater Project.
Reproduction Courtesy of the Prints and Photographs
Division, Library of Congress, Washington, D.C.

Postwar Era and a Gathering Storm

With an improved economy in the decades following World War II, artists shifted their attentions. Modernism in the form of abstraction came to dominate the art world. And while the reduction of artists' political engagement was partially due to art world fashion, the anti-communist backlash of the Cold War had a much more sinister impact.

The McCarthy Era witch hunts of the late 1940s intimidated many politically-aware artists and discouraged a new generation from making political art. Artists, along with those in the entertainment industry, educators, union members, activists and government employees, became the subject of aggressive investigations and questioning. An individual who had been issued a subpoena to appear before government panels and committees was required to name alleged communist sympathizers. Both those named and those refusing to "name names" wound up on a "do not hire" or "blacklist" that deprived them of their livelihoods. Countless victims suffered destruction of their careers, imprisonment, with many committing suicide or fleeing the country to avoid becoming "stool pigeons."

In 1953, Jacob Burck had deportation hearings initiated against him by the US Immigration Service, which accused him of belonging to the Communist Party. By that time he was a Pulitzer Prize-winning illustrator for the *Chicago Times*. Charges were eventually dropped.

Rockwell Kent's popularity declined from its heights in the 1930s due in part to his support of radical causes. In the 1950s the State Department revoked his passport, refusing to issue passports to Communists and their sympathizers. Many blacklisted US political refugees fled to Mexico which would accept US citizens without the passports denied them by the US Government.[32] Rockwell Kent's case went to the Supreme Court. He opposed the State Department's claim of authority to revoke passports based on political association. The case was decided in Kent's favor in 1958 on free speech grounds.[33]

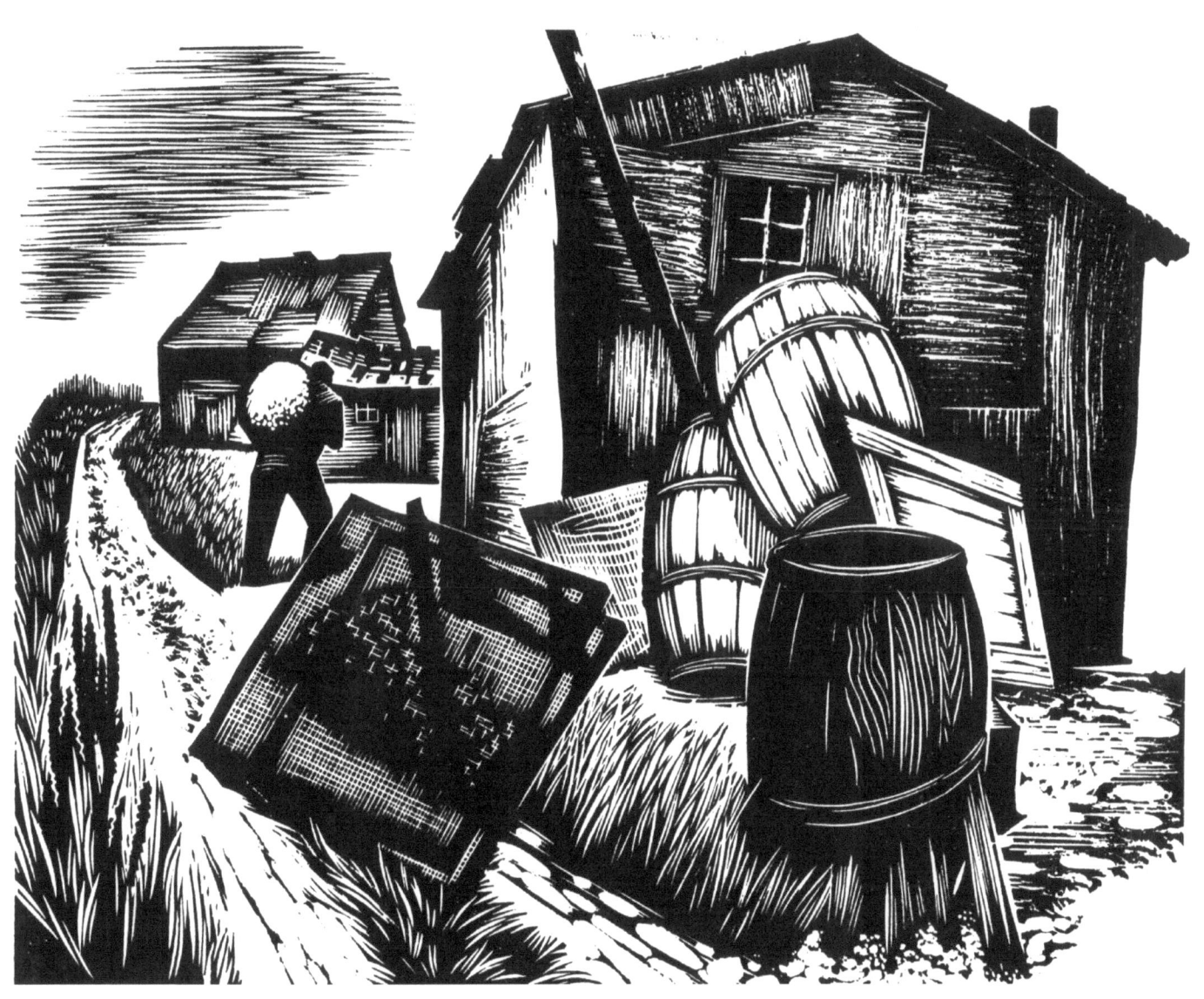

Figure 11.
Richard V. Correll
(1904-1990)
Dwellings of the Jobless #3, 1939
Linocut, 8 x 10"
Reproduction Courtesy of Estate of Richard V. Correll

Anton Refregier's Treasury Section mural in San Francisco (figure #35) had been delayed by World War II so that by the time he completed it in 1949, the political climate had turned strongly anti-communist and he was forced to repaint parts that were found offensive to the new conservative era. The mural is the last project of the New Deal art programs. Government officials responsible for the mural did not allow him to include a portrait of FDR. While painting, he was threatened by angry groups that gathered to harass him. After completion, the mural survived attempts to destroy it by then-Congressman Richard Nixon and others.[34]

Even if not overt, the pressure of the times affected artists. Richard V. Correll (figure #11) had been active in the WPA/FAP in the Northwest. After he moved to New York during World War II, he was on the board of the Artists League of America, an organization of progressive artists that was descended from the American Artists' Congress and headed by Rockwell Kent. But by the 1950s he found an art world dominated by abstraction and a changed political environment, all of which contributed to his move to San Francisco.[35]

While many artists persisted in their activism and social commentary, the changing tide forced them to operate increasingly at the margins of the art world.

Fritz Eichenberg (figure #12) who had fled Germany when the Nazi Party came to power in 1933, began teaching wood engraving at the New School for Social Research and creating images for the WPA/FAP, as well as for the *Nation*. His pacifism led him to convert from Judaism to the Quaker religion. In 1953, he met the co-founder of the Catholic Worker Movement, Dorothy Day. Her dedication to fighting poverty convinced him to become a contributor to the *Catholic Worker* newspaper.

The Catholic Worker Movement originated during the Depression. The newspaper began publishing in 1933 with a focus on the social teachings of the church and advocating for the poor and displaced workers. The first Catholic Worker House of Hospitality for transient or homeless persons was established with a small apartment in New York. From there, the Hospitality House movement spread across the country in a spontaneous way. Today many Hospitality Houses are independent entities not necessarily connected to the Catholic Worker Movement.[36]

Eichenberg's image of a breadline with Christ standing in shared suffering speaks to the role of religion as a witness to homelessness. It also points to the way artists and activists can work together. Eichenberg created wood engravings for the *Catholic Worker* at no charge for many years. But Eichenberg's wood engravings stand practically alone for a period of decades in their commentary on poverty. This is partially due to the suppression of political art, but another factor was the increasing invisibility of homelessness in America.

At the same time the country was shifting toward Cold War politics and abstraction it also was becoming prosperous. A broadening of educational opportunity was at least part of the cause. The GI Bill or Serviceman's Readjustment Act of 1944 provided college or vocational education for returning World War II veterans as well as a year of unemployment compensation. This encouraged massive growth in the education sector, leading to an unparalleled broadening of the middle-class. The result was an unprecedented narrowing of economic disparity.[37]

In the 1960s, President Lyndon Johnson's War on Poverty programs further reduced poverty in the elderly and the disabled through Medicare and Medicaid. Civil Rights legislation reduced economic disparity for a time as well.

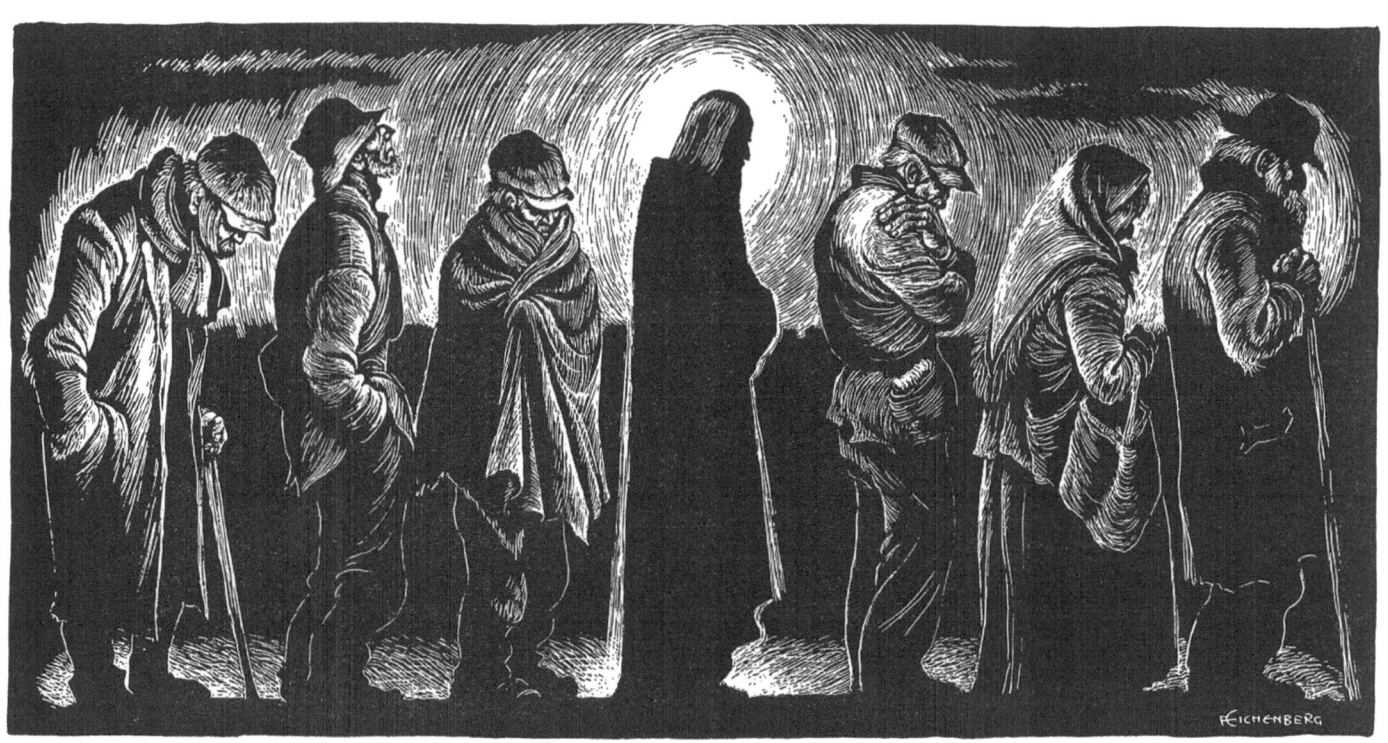

FRITZ EICHENBERG © 1952

Figure 12.
Fritz Eichenberg
(1901-1990)
Christ of the Breadline, 1953
Wood Engraving, 13 3/4 x 9"
Art © Fritz Eichenberg Trust/Licensed by VAGA, New York, NY
Collection of University of Rhode Island Library Special Collections

A Disaster in the Making

During this period of widening prosperity, a series of negative factors influenced the face of homelessness.

Hopping free rides on trains had become a part of hobo life in the 19th century. Until late in the 1950s, it provided a means of mobility for poor people in search of work. But as access to trains became more difficult and security in the rail yards more intense, the rail gradually disappeared as a form of transport for them. The result was increased isolation and restricted movement for many poor people.

In addition, cities began to close in on neighborhoods that had traditionally been home to poor people. Many of them were increasingly cut off from job opportunities. They couldn't ride the rails, itinerant work was becoming more structured, and the population in these areas was aging rapidly. With such a ripe target, city governments all over the country began "redeveloping" these neighborhoods. Redevelopment meant displacement for retired and poor workers. And there was nowhere for many of them to go.

Redevelopment and Urban Renewal

With the post-war prosperity of the late 1940s, redevelopment and urban renewal became the focus of cities around the country. In order to house an expanding middle-class, the federal government gave tax incentives that aided in the demolition of neighborhoods and the displacement of huge numbers of poor people.

Minorities made up 75% of people displaced nationwide due to urban renewal projects in the 20th century. From Atlanta, to Kansas City, from Pittsburgh, to Boston, a series of infamous urban renewal projects destroyed poor communities. The dislocation resulted in broken support networks, eviscerated cultural ties and increased instability for thousands of people.[38] The alliances that had formed between the working class and the unemployed poor during Roosevelt's time were severed, weakening the movement toward equity. Deliberate attempts to split this alliance became increasingly more apparent. But so too did the resistance.

In 1953, San Francisco's Western Addition became the target of one of the largest urban renewal projects in the West, encompassing hundreds of city blocks and impacting close to 20,000 residents. Groups organized to fight back and Western Addition Community Organization (WACO) was founded in 1967 to fight against displacement.

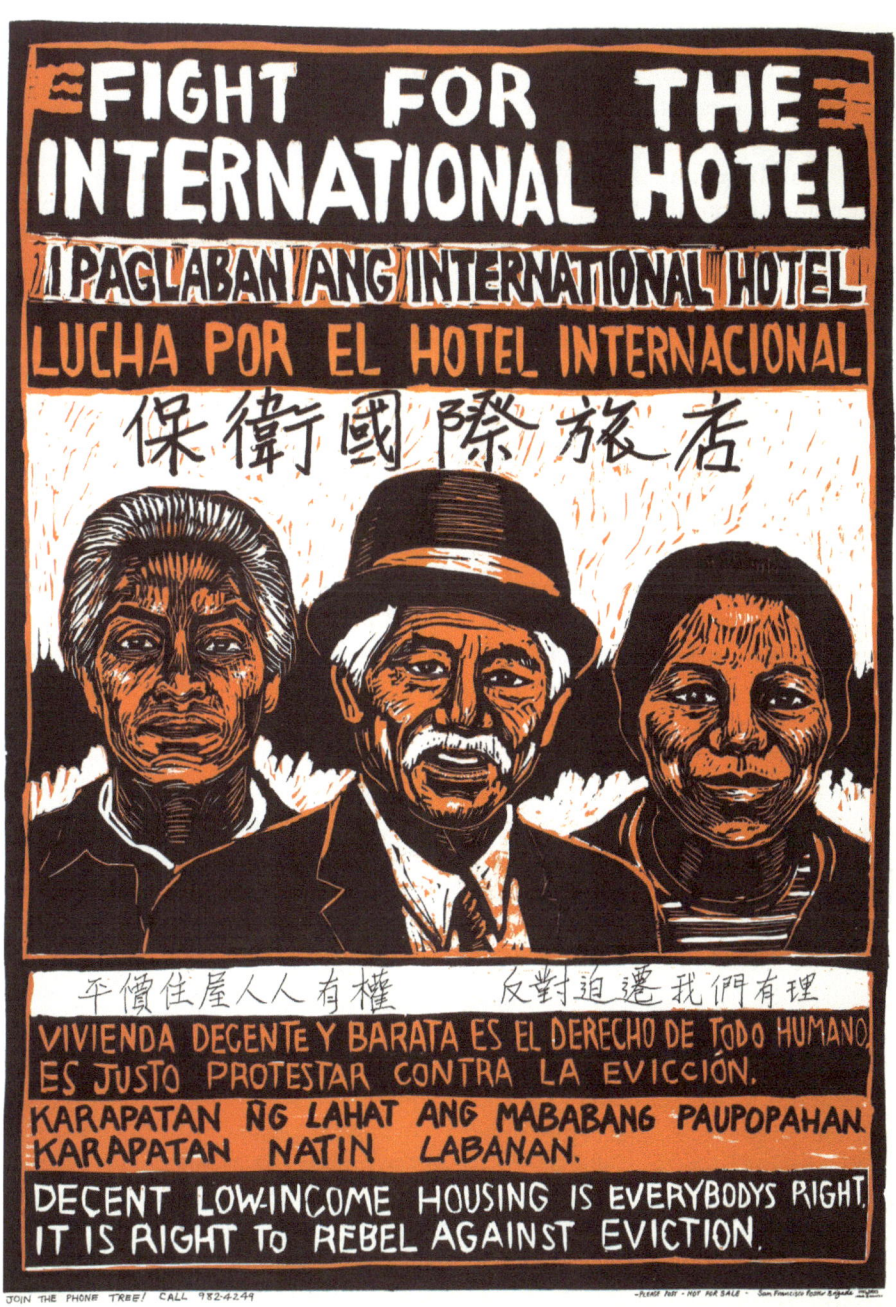

Nearly a decade later, a similar struggle to prevent redevelopment from destroying housing and displacing poor residents took place at the International Hotel or I-Hotel in San Francisco, home to fifty elderly tenants, one of the last remnants of the Filipino community known as "Little Manila." Between 1975 and 1984, the San Francisco Poster Brigade designed hundreds of political posters. Rachael Bell (now Rachael Romero) was the principal artist of the Poster Brigade. They created posters to protest the demolition of the hotel. People organized to fight the demolition from 1968 until 1977, when the building was stormed in the middle of the night by 400 police in full riot gear.

The builder who evicted the tenants went bankrupt and the lot remained undeveloped for over 20 years. In a bittersweet victory, a new building called I-Hotel Manilatown Center has been constructed at the site.[39]

Romero says of her poster (figure #13), "I had become a close friend of Felix Ayson, who is in the center of the poster. A wonderful man, thoughtful, articulate with an independent mind, he was one of the main speakers on behalf of the tenants. Next to Felix in the poster is another of the tenant leaders, What Tampao. On the other side is Mrs. Aquino. One of the few women living in the Hotel, she also became a spokesperson for the tenants. The Tagalog and the Chinese was written out for me to copy into the design. The posters were wheat pasted all over the city."

Deinstitutionalization

Another structural shift pushed more and more people into homelessness and the streets. Beginning in the 1960s and continuing on into the 1980s, there was a movement to close the huge and often inhumane mental health hospitals across the country and replace them with new and smaller neighborhood-based mental health facilities. Well-meaning people who saw the horrible conditions of many of these hospitals called for their closure, but many politicians saw it as an opportunity for cutting state expenditures. The widespread closure of public health mental hospitals was accomplished, but the new facilities were either never built or were vastly under-funded. The process led to thousands of people being dumped on the street.

During his time as governor of California, Ronald Reagan pushed through a policy of deinstitutionalization. During his administration, patients at state mental hospitals decreased from 26,500 in 1967 to 6,400 in 1974. Replacement care facilities were slow in coming, if they came at all. As president, Reagan continued this policy by devolving care to the states, which were eager to severely cut the programs.[40] Today the largest mental health facility in California is the Los Angeles County Jail. According to a 2007 study by the US Justice Department, 64 percent of inmates across the country reported mental health problems.[41] Mass incarceration has simply replaced the mental health hospitals, while those on the outside are offered fewer treatment options.[42]

By the late 1970s cities and Chambers of Commerce across the country were celebrating their final victories in displacing poor people. They believed they had swept the destitute away, made them disappear. However the 1980s represented the beginning of the blowback for their policies and the return of massive homelessness. A return to fiscally-conservative ideology and other structural changes in the American economy began a period of increased poverty and economic inequality. The philosophy of government's role had shifted so that social programs of all kinds were redefined as a burden on the American taxpayer, a handout for lazy people and eventually as itself a cause of poverty.

With the election in 1980 of Ronald Reagan as president, the assault began on New Deal and Great Society policies using anti-government rhetoric and theories of "trickle down" economics. The policies that had made the era since World War II the most economically egalitarian in US history were systematically removed. Federal funding of social programs was slashed. Affordable housing production came to a stand still. Together, these factors left millions of people without economic security, unable to afford housing, and eventually out on the streets. During the 1980s, homelessness tripled or quadrupled in many US cities.[43]

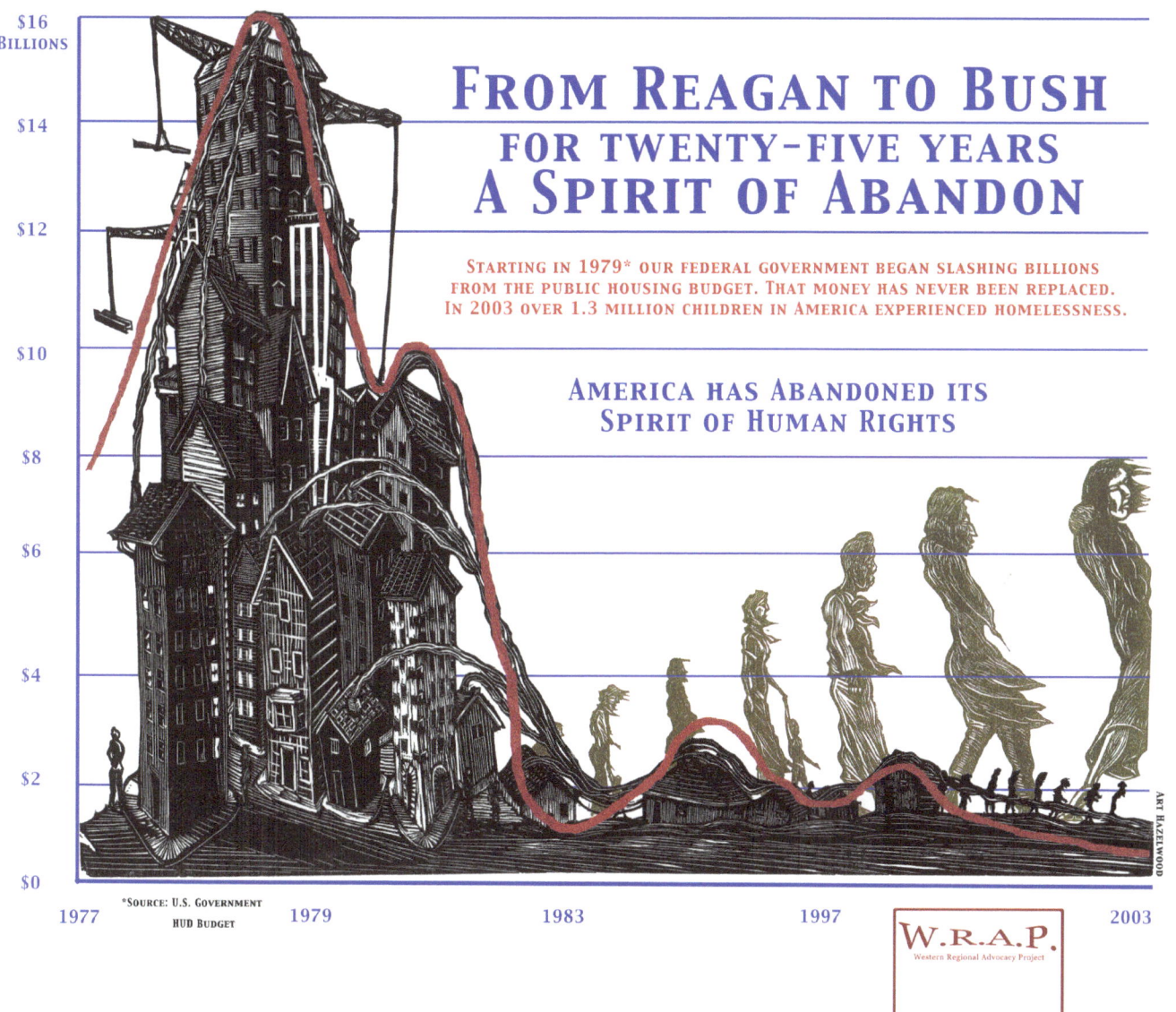

FROM REAGAN TO BUSH
FOR TWENTY-FIVE YEARS
A SPIRIT OF ABANDON

STARTING IN 1979* OUR FEDERAL GOVERNMENT BEGAN SLASHING BILLIONS
FROM THE PUBLIC HOUSING BUDGET. THAT MONEY HAS NEVER BEEN REPLACED.
IN 2003 OVER 1.3 MILLION CHILDREN IN AMERICA EXPERIENCED HOMELESSNESS.

AMERICA HAS ABANDONED ITS
SPIRIT OF HUMAN RIGHTS

$16 BILLIONS
$14
$12
$10
$8
$6
$4
$2
$0

*SOURCE: U.S. GOVERNMENT HUD BUDGET

1977   1979   1983   1997   2003

ART HAZELWOOD

W.R.A.P.
Western Regional Advocacy Project

Figure 14.
Art Hazelwood
(1961-)
Spirit of Abandon, 2006
Screen Print, 18 x 21"
Reproduction Courtesy of the Artist
Loaned for the exhibition by Western Regional Advocacy Project

31

Contempory Artists Respond

As poverty and homelessness again became visible in cities across the US, artists started to respond to the crisis. By the 1980s the dominance of abstract art had waned as had the power of anticommunist rhetoric to inspire fear. Artists began again to use a wide range of tools to communicate political content, although they faced a more divided art world, and minimal government support for what the New Deal administrators had called, "democratic culture."

In 2006, the Western Regional Advocacy Project (WRAP) produced *Without Housing: Decades of Federal Housing Cutbacks, Massive Homelessness and Policy Failures,* a report that pointed out the policies the federal government has pursued since the early 1980s to sharply reduce funding for affordable housing. The report uses artwork to portray the statistical data. In *Spirit of Abandon*, (figure #14) Art Hazelwood represents the dwindling funds for public housing as ever-shrinking buildings, while the rise in homelessness is represented by larger and larger human figures. The year 1983 represents the deepest federal cuts to funding for affordable housing and marks the beginning of contemporary homelessness.

WRAP brings together grassroots groups in the western US to address wider issues of federal and state policies that affect homeless people. Many of the homeless rights groups are too busy dealing with local issues to have time for the bigger picture. WRAP is an example of an organization that seeks to bring artists into their activist realm. It is a mutually beneficial union: artistic imagery can help educate and build the emotional commitment of members and of the public. In turn, by working with these organizations, artists gain a deeper understanding of the issues. The relationship also provides artists with a wider audience for their messages.

The San Francisco *Street Sheet,* (figures #15, 16) is the oldest continuously published newspaper about homelessness in the US. It began in 1989 as the publication of the Coalition on Homelessness. The American Friends Service Committee has published the *Street Spirit* (figures #17, 18) based in Oakland, California since 1996. Both papers have always used paintings, cartoons, woodcuts, screenprints and drawings that address issues of economic justice and homelessness. The papers draw attention to the struggle for dignity and human rights by low-income and poor people facing eviction, homelessness, psychiatric treatment and other issues. They report from the shelters,

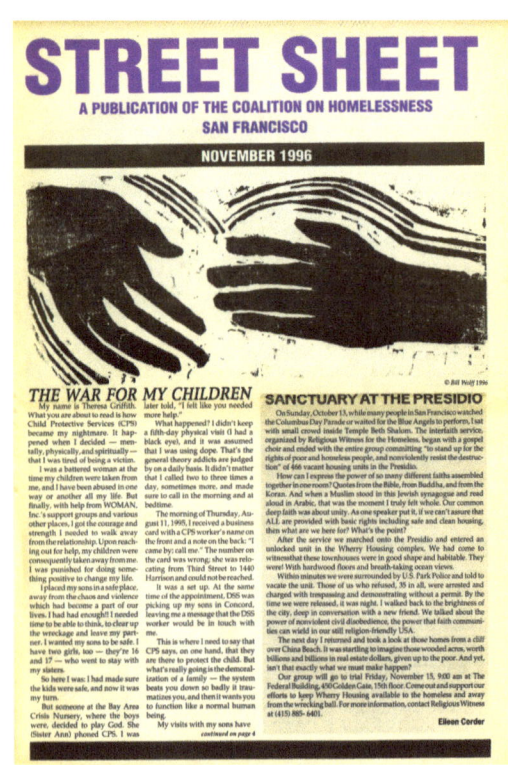

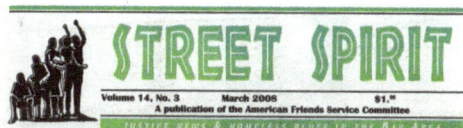

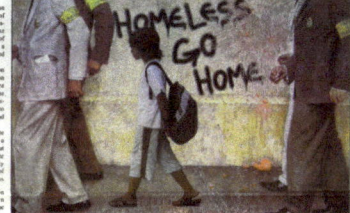

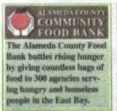

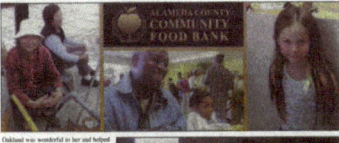

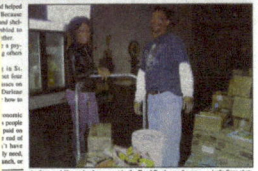

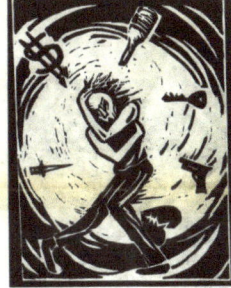

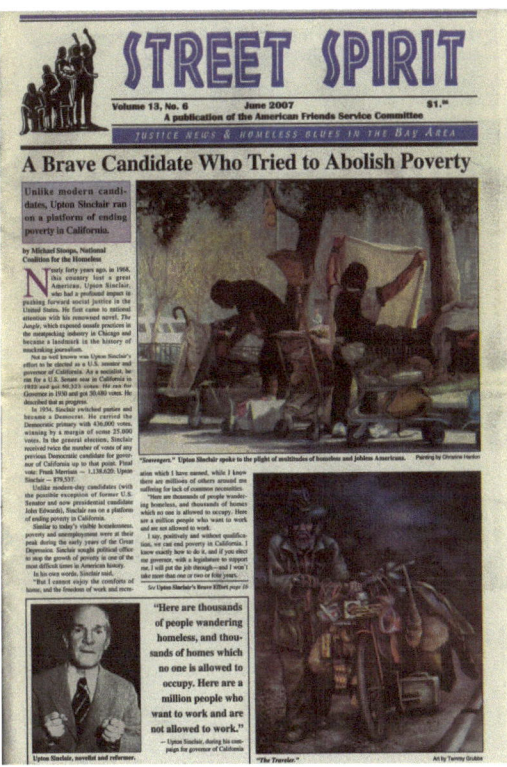

Figure 15.
Street Sheet
November 1996, cover image by William F. Wolff, 17 x 11"

Figure 16.
Street Sheet
May 1998, cover image by Eliza Miller, 17 x 11"

Figure 17.
Street Spirit
March 2008, cover image by Nili Yosha, 17 x 11"

Figure 18.
Street Spirit
June 2007, cover images by Christine Hanlon (top),
Tammy Grubbs (bottom), 17 x 11"

soup kitchens and SRO hotels where the mainstream press rarely visits. The papers are sold by homeless vendors. There are now twenty three street papers in the US. All these papers have access to a shared internet archive of artwork that addresses homelessness, another way to broaden the reach of imagery.

Artists have also been able to communicate social issues through mainstream magazines. Eric Drooker is an artist whose path has taken him from street artist to illustrator for publications that include *The New Yorker*, (figure #19, 20) the *Village Voice* and the *Nation*. His artwork counteracts negative views of homeless people with images that often verge on the ecstatic. Not many artists have been able to imbue the struggle of poor people with the nearly euphoric enthusiasm that Drooker does. He communicates something similar to the free spirit in poverty expressed by Charlie Chaplin or by Jack Keruoac in *On the Road*.

Posters play a much more visible role in the recent era. The use of the poster as a way to disseminate a political message began in earnest in the 1960s, with a focus on third world struggles, the war in Vietnam and civil rights. The issue of poverty and specifically homelessness was not well represented in this period. Only later in the 1990s, as it became increasingly evident that widespread homelessness was a result of government divestment and the privatization of public space, did posters begin to address this reality. Following in the tradition

of the San Francisco Poster Brigade, the San Francisco Print Collective (SFPC) was founded in 2000 by a group of artists with the purpose of using graphic art to support social justice organizing. The SFPC uses screenprint posters, banners, and murals created in collaboration with organizations like the Coalition on Homelessness and the Mission Anti-displacement Coalition. In 2006, they worked with Northern California War Tax Resistance to create a poster campaign that exposes federal spending priorities in a time of war. *33% of Homeless Are Veterans* (figure #21) was created for that campaign to draw attention to the estimated number of homeless people that are veterans.

Even so, ambivalence about homelessness as a proper political issue persisted among the left. The split among left groups was reinforced by right wing propaganda regarding "trickle down" economics and bootstrap individualism, and by media that dehumanizes and scapegoats homeless people. During the 1990s in "liberal" San Francisco, the daily newspapers waged a sustained campaign to portray the visible presence of homeless people in the midst of residential and commercial neighborhoods as a blight that threatened, commerce, property values and the "quality of life" for everyone else.[44]

But hostility on the left exists as well, perhaps as a hangover of Marx's dismissal of "social scum (Lumpenproletartiat)."[45] In 2010, for example, Mike Rotkin, the self-avowed "socialist feminist" mayor of the city of Santa Cruz and a teacher of Marxist theory at the University of California at Santa Cruz, called for criminalizing homeless people by outlawing sitting on sidewalks and supporting other anti-homeless measures.[46] He is not

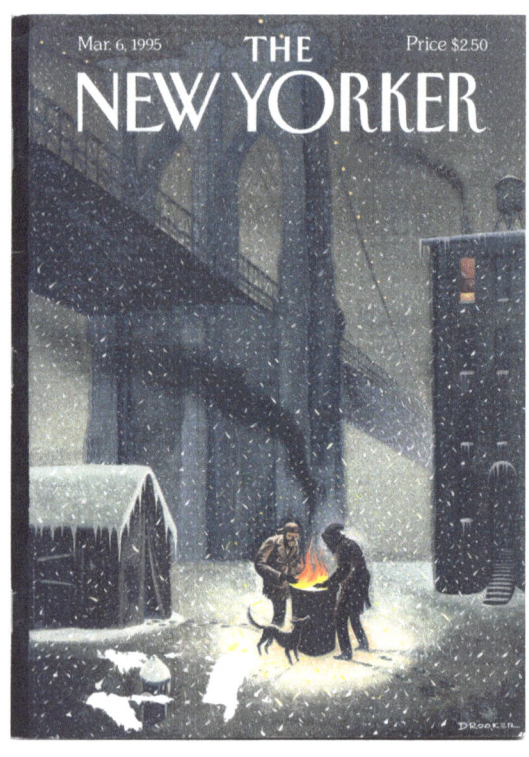

Figure 19.
Eric Drooker
(1958-)
Under Bridges,
The New Yorker,
March 1995, 11 x 8"

alone among liberal politicians. Nation-wide, cities across the political spectrum have passed anti-homeless laws, and continue to use anti-homeless rhetoric and policies as election strategies.

Not until fairly recently has homelessness reemerged in the US as a human rights issue. The right to adequate housing was first placed on the international human rights agenda in the Universal Declaration of Human Rights that was drafted by a committee chaired by Eleanor Roosevelt.[47]

The contemporary artwork depicted in this book and exhibition represents a turn towards acknowledging the truth of the 1948 UN Declaration: that housing is a human right. In 2009, homeless rights organizations presented work by several of these artists as testimony to the United Nations Special Rapporteur on housing who toured the US gathering information about violations of housing as a basic human right.

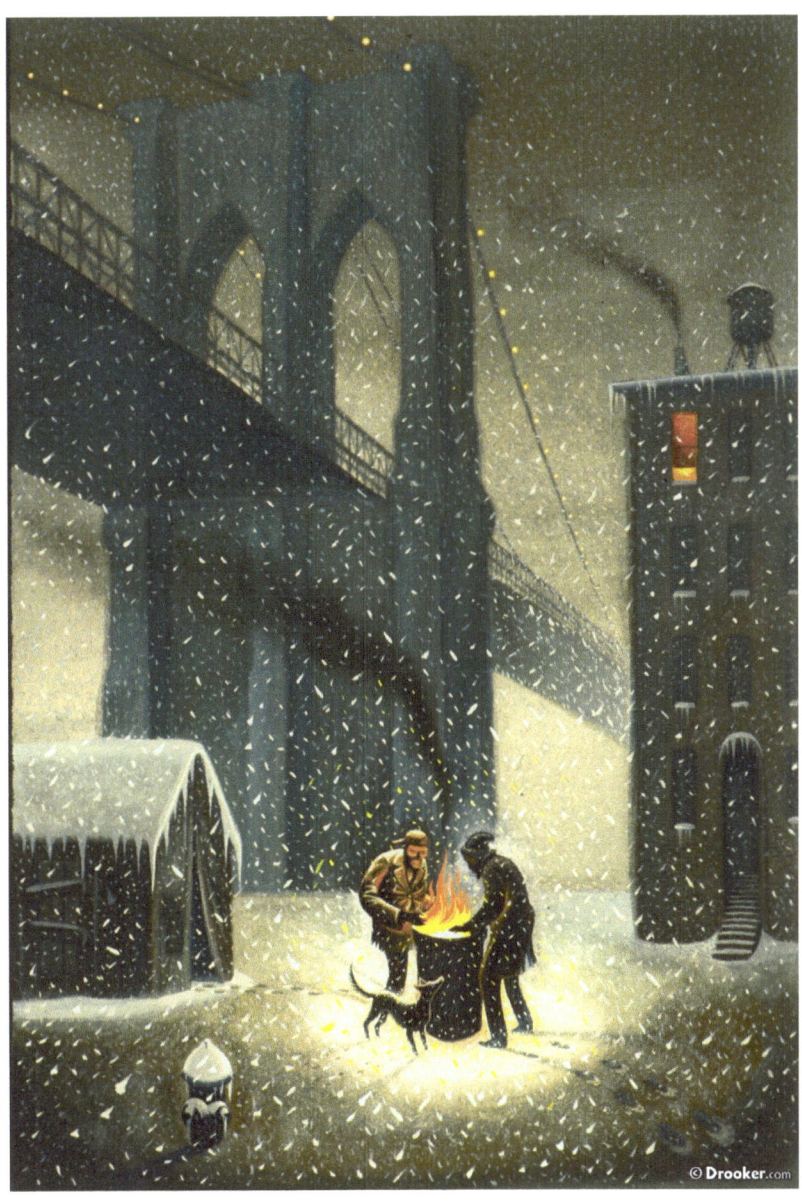

Figure 20.
Eric Drooker
(1958-)
Under Bridges, 1995
Painting, 11 x 15"
Reproduction Courtesy of the Artist

35

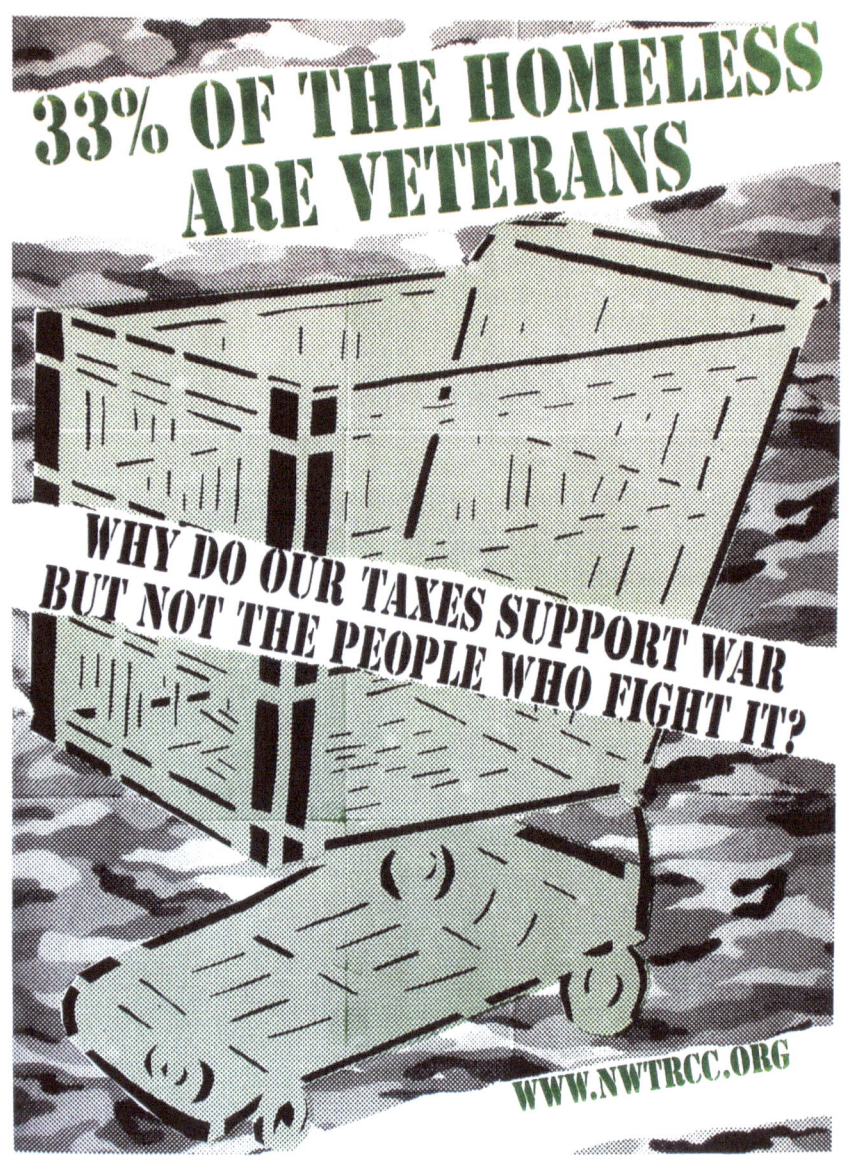

33% OF THE HOMELESS ARE VETERANS

WHY DO OUR TAXES SUPPORT WAR BUT NOT THE PEOPLE WHO FIGHT IT?

WWW.NWTRCC.ORG

Everyone has the right to a standard of living adequate for the health and well-being of himself and of his family, including food, clothing, housing and medical care and necessary social services, and the right to security in the event of unemployment, sickness, disability, widowhood, old age or other lack of livelihood in circumstances beyond his control.

Universal Declaration of Human Rights
Article 25, Section (1), 1948

Figure 21.
San Francisco Print Collective
33% of Homeless are Veterans, 2006
Screen Print, 22 x 16 1/2"
Reproduction Courtesy of the SFPC

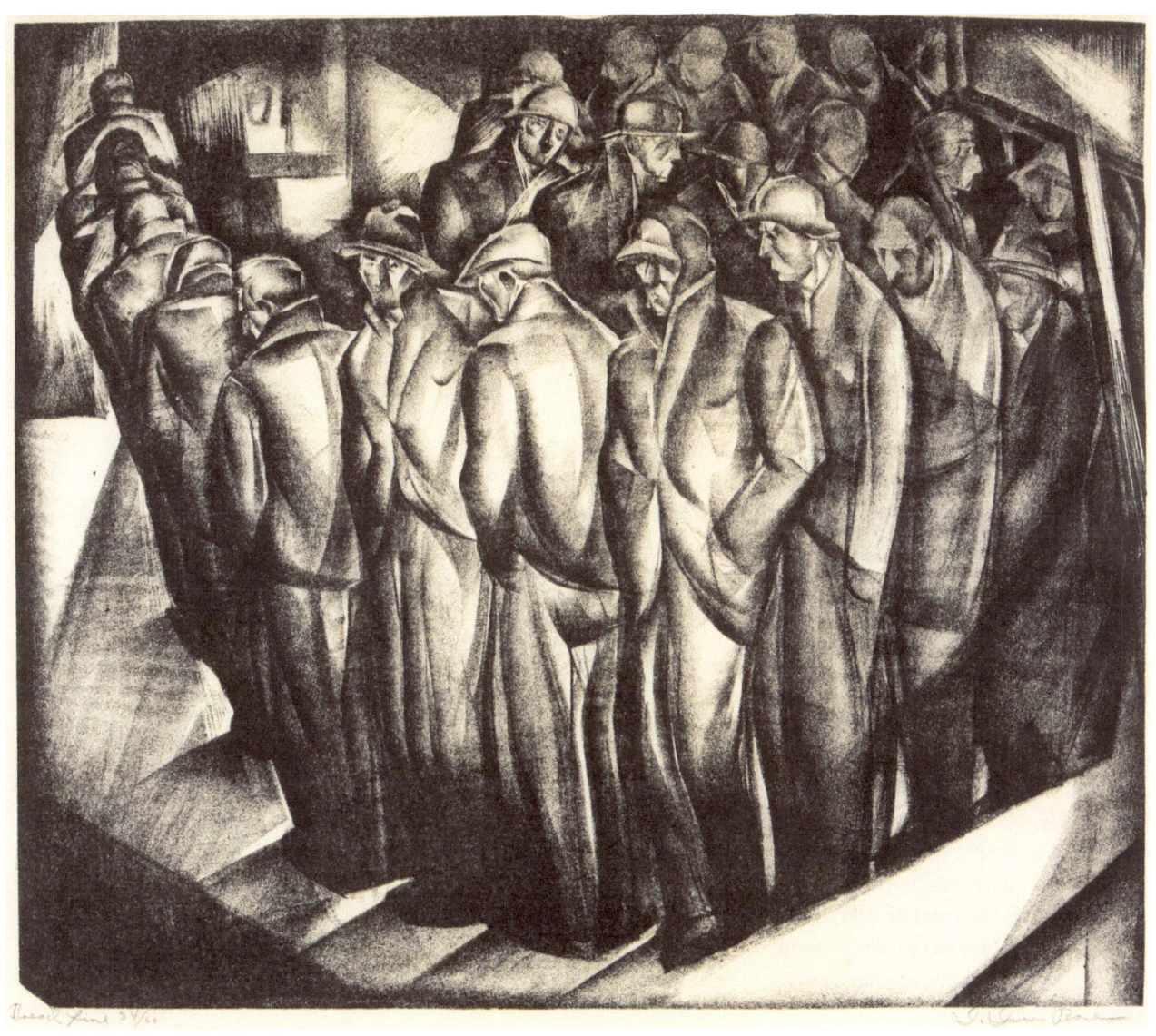

Figure 22.
Iver Rose
(1899-1972)
Bread Line, 1935
Lithograph, 15 x 17 3/8"
From the Collection of M. Lee Stone Fine
Prints, San Jose, CA
Photo Credit: Robert Berger Photography

Iver Rose worked for a time as a commercial artist in New York but moved back to his hometown of Chicago during the Depression. The Cubist distortions in his work illustrate that the line between socially engaged art and Modernism were not as clear cut in the 1930s as many claim. In almost all depictions of breadlines during the Depression, including in photographs, the lines are made up entirely of men.

Daily Realities

Breadlines and soup kitchens, panhandling and finding shelter, scavenging and dumpster diving make up the daily realities of life in extreme poverty. Meeting the basic necessities can consume all of one's energy. The struggle just to survive another day with one's pride intact is often overlooked by people who see only a "problem population."

Both Depression-era and contemporary artists offer glimpses of life on the street that show many similarities between the eras. Images of breadlines such as those by Iver Rose (figure #22) and Clare Leighton (figure #26) use expressive techniques to emphasize the magnitude of the issue. The distortion in both images creates a sense that the numbers of those seeking assistance is unlimited and therefore implicitly call for action. In contrast, Kiki Smith's 2006 print, *Home,* (figure #23) focuses on a single individual. The image expresses the shock of seeing a person at "home" in a box, and yet the realities of homelessness today are more ingrained in our society than at any time since the Great Depression. More and more Americans don't remember a time when it wasn't commonplace to see many people living on the street.

The print by Isac Friedlander (figure #25) made in 1932 portrays the struggle of making a living on the street off the waste of other people. In the Depression, it was a pushcart; today it is a shopping cart. It is ironic that this American basket of plenty has become the symbol of homelessness. In Christine Hanlon's painting, (figure #24) the shopping cart has become a means of providing for the basics of survival as the people in the painting push their loads toward a recycling center.

Figure 23.
Kiki Smith
(1954-)
Home, 2006
Color spit bite aquatint with flat bite, hard ground and soft ground etching, and drypoint printed on gampi paper chine collé
26 1/2 x 31" Edition of 20
© Kiki Smith, courtesy The Pace Gallery
Loaned for the exhibition by Crown Point Press

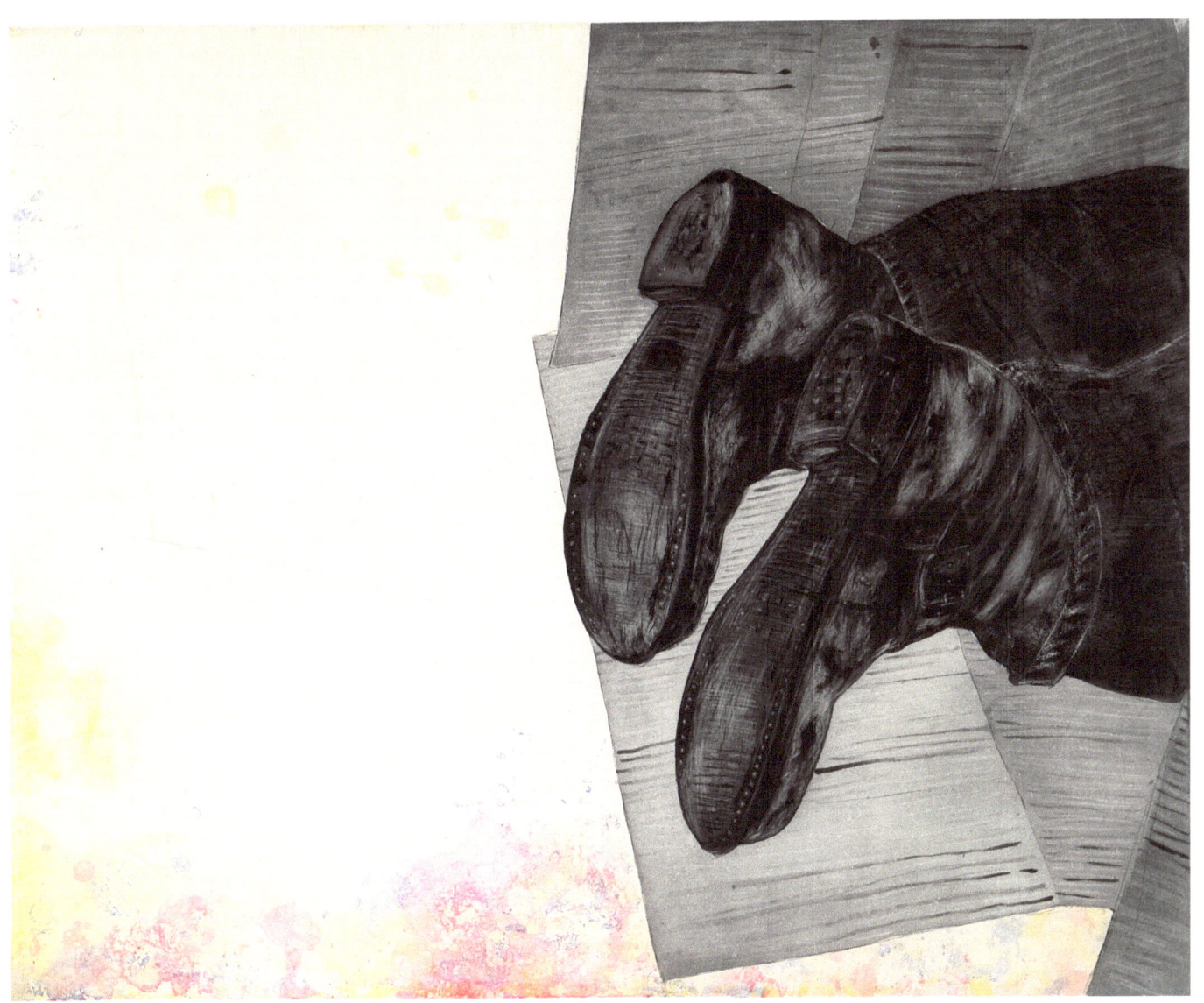

Kiki Smith was having a one person show at the San Francisco Museum of Modern Art when she created this print at Crown Point Press in San Francisco. The willingness of such a well-respected artist to approach a "difficult" subject speaks to the change that the art world has undergone. The school of thought that emerged from the Cold War era and that continued to marginalize and dismiss political art was becoming increasingly difficult to justify.

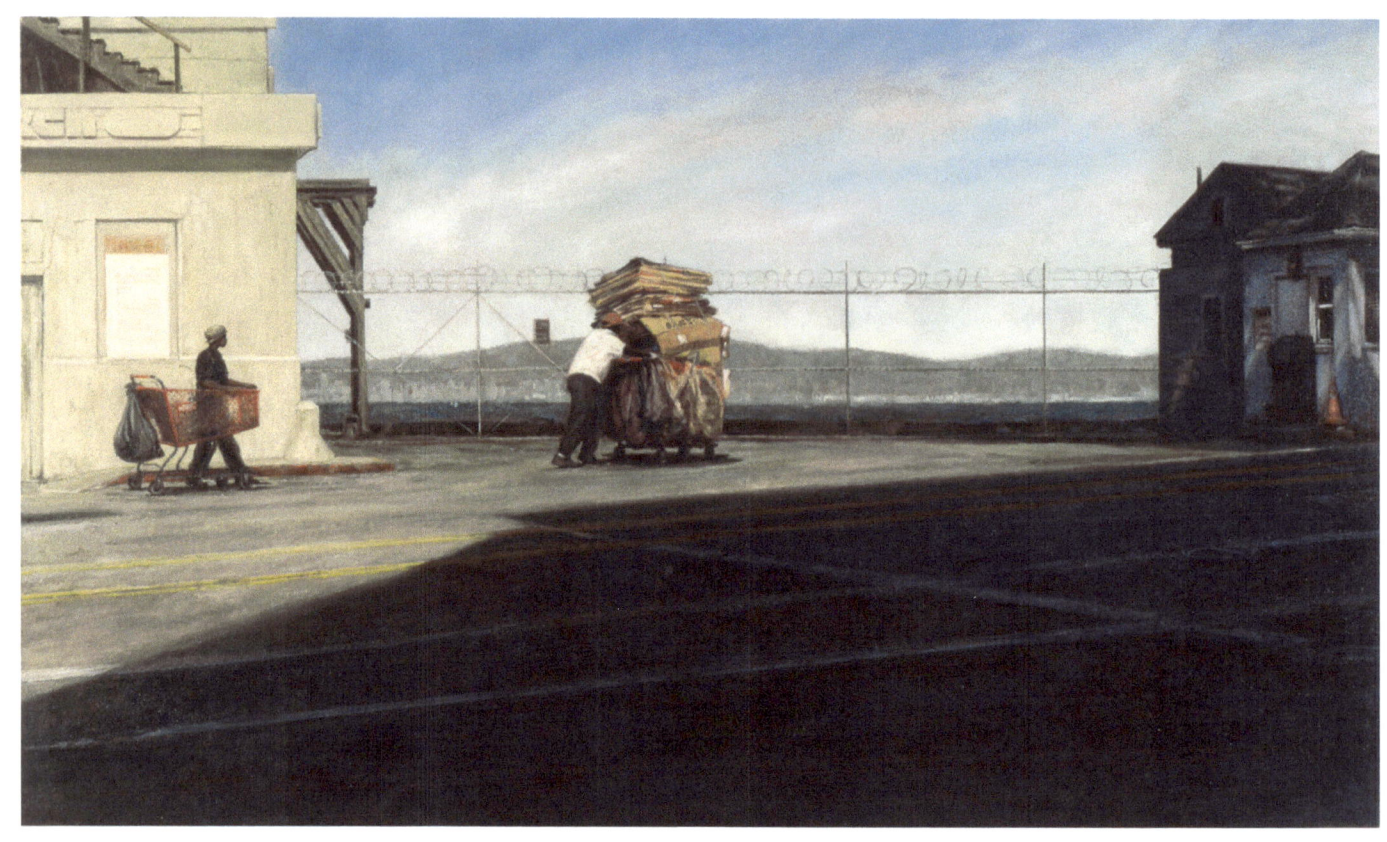

Figure 24.
Christine Hanlon
(1954-)
Third Street Corridor, 1998
Oil on Canvas, 30 x 52"
Reproduction Courtesy of the Artist

Hanlon says of this painting, "Traditional cityscapes don't include the homeless so I wanted to create an opportunity for the viewer to consider the issues around homelessness and contemplate the reality of life on the street, without the concurrent guilt, pity or avoidance that real life encounters may provoke."

Figure 25.
Isac Friedlander
(1890-1968)
Golddigger, 1932
Wood Engraving, 5 x 3 3/8"
Reproduction courtesy of the estate of
isac Friedlander
From the Collection of M. Lee Stone Fine
Prints, San Jose, CA
Photo Credit: Robert Berger Photography

Friedlander was born in Latvia. At
sixteen he was arrested for involvement in the murder of his teacher and
served four-years in a military prison.
After his release he went to Italy where
he studied printmaking and painting
at the Academy of Rome. In 1929, at
the beginning of the Depression, he
immigrated to America where he produced many wood engravings.

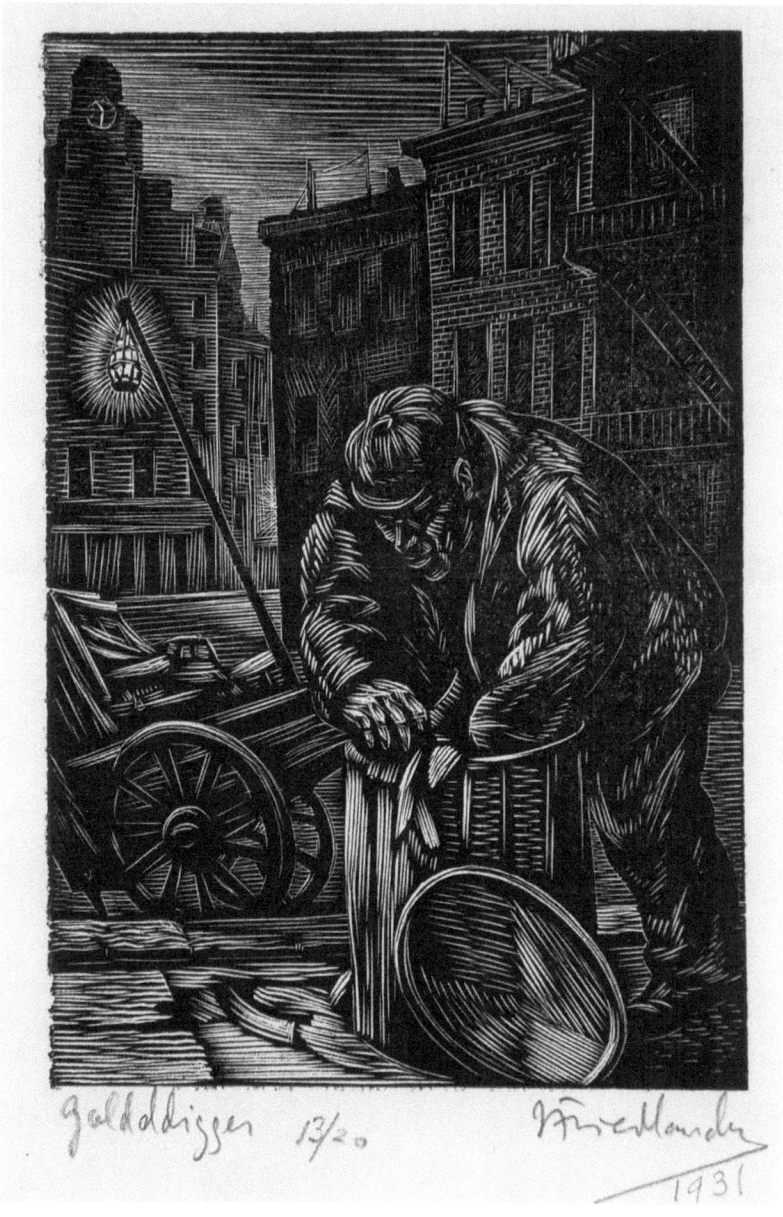

Figure 26.
Clare Leighton
(c 1898-1989)
Bread Line, 1932
Wood Engraving, 12 x 8"
Reproduction with permission from the estate of Claire Leighton
From the Collection of M. Lee Stone Fine Prints, San Jose, CA
Photo Credit: Robert Berger Photography

After several teaching trips to the US, London-born Clare Leighton immigrated in 1938. She was an artist, writer and illustrator who, like Fritz Eichenberg, illustrated several literary texts. She was among a handful of artists that revived the media of wood engraving and turned what had been a reproductive technique into an artistically expressive one.

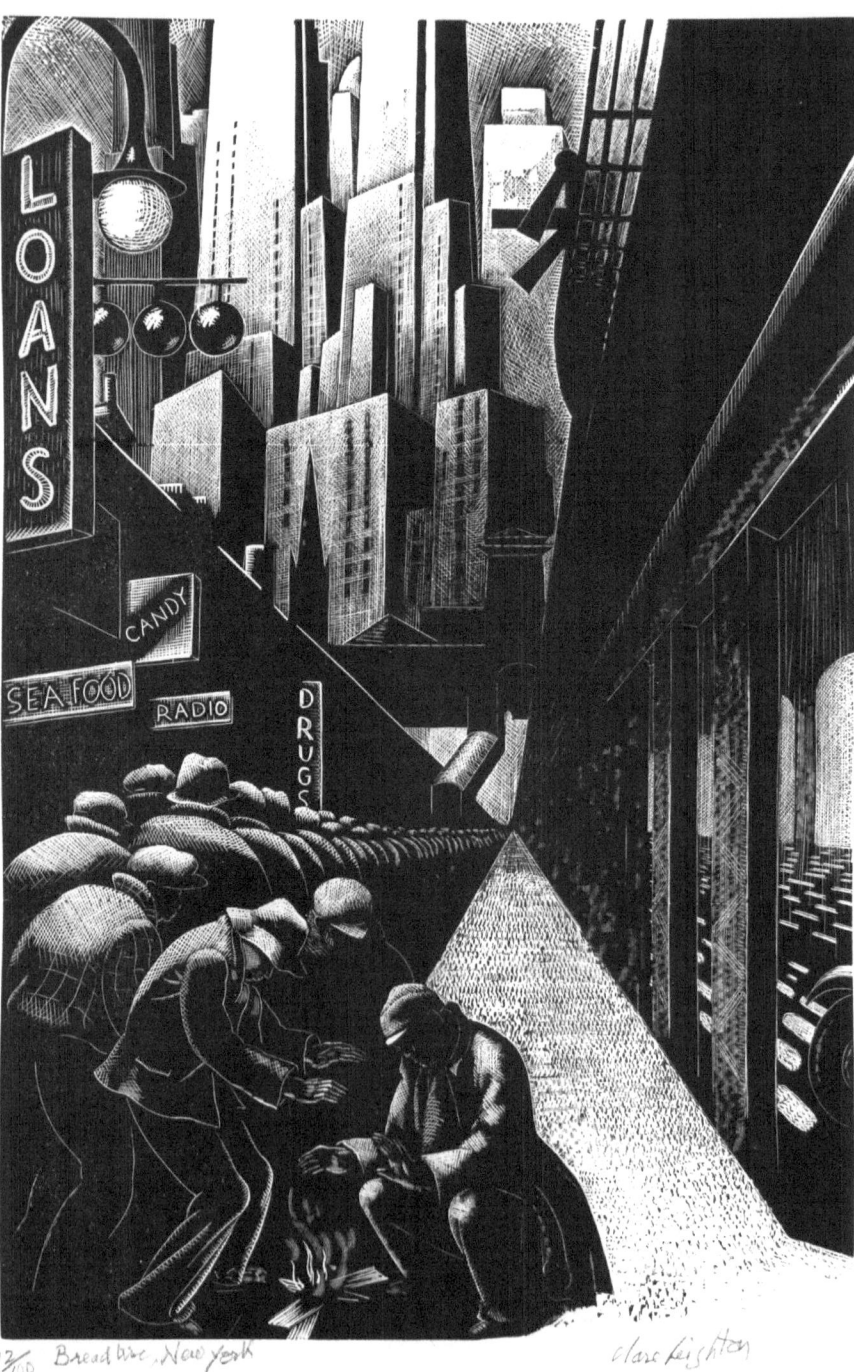

42

Figure 27.
Eric Drooker
(1958-)
Flood! A Novel in Pictures, 1992, 9 x 6 1/4"

The book, *Flood!*, is a graphic novel without words. The first section is titled "Home" and tells the story of a man losing his job, then his apartment, and then wandering the streets of New York. He temporarily escapes into a fantasy of tribal unity, only to be awakened from his dream by the police and told to move on.

This graphic novel without words revives a tradition that was quite popular in the 1920s and 30s by artists such as Frans Masereel, Lynd Ward, and Giacomo Patri (figures #6, 7, 8, 9) whose book *White Collar* explores similar themes as Drooker's.

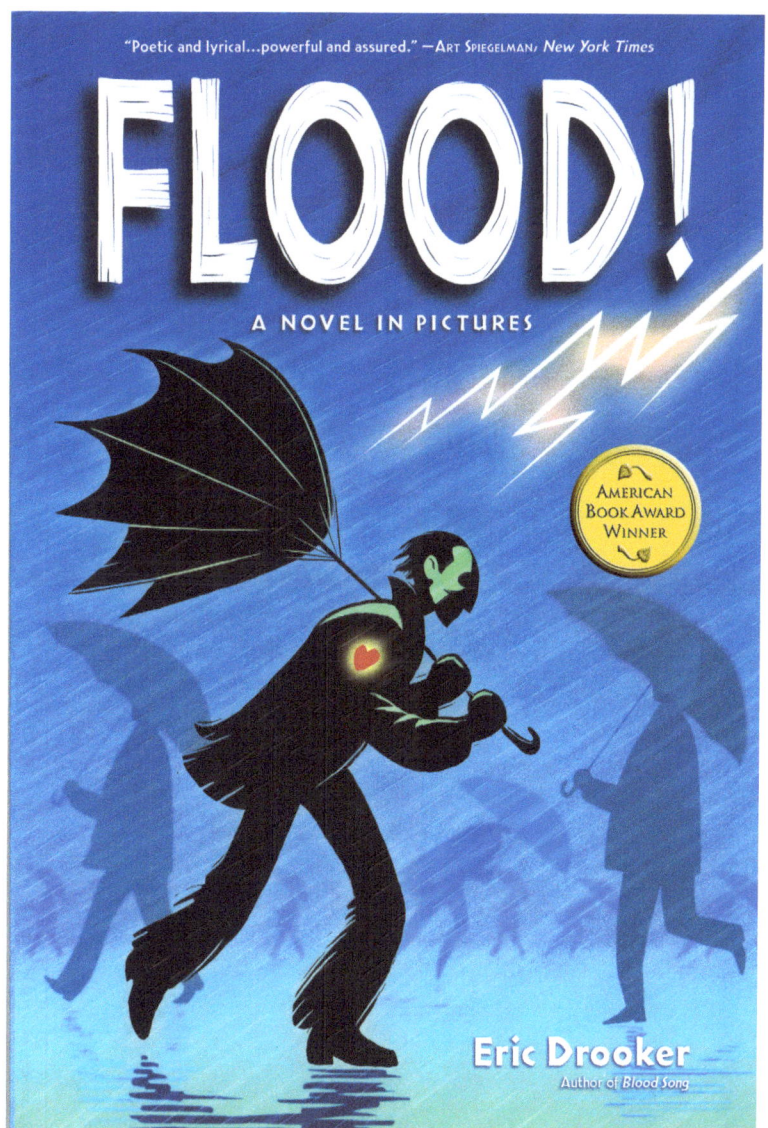

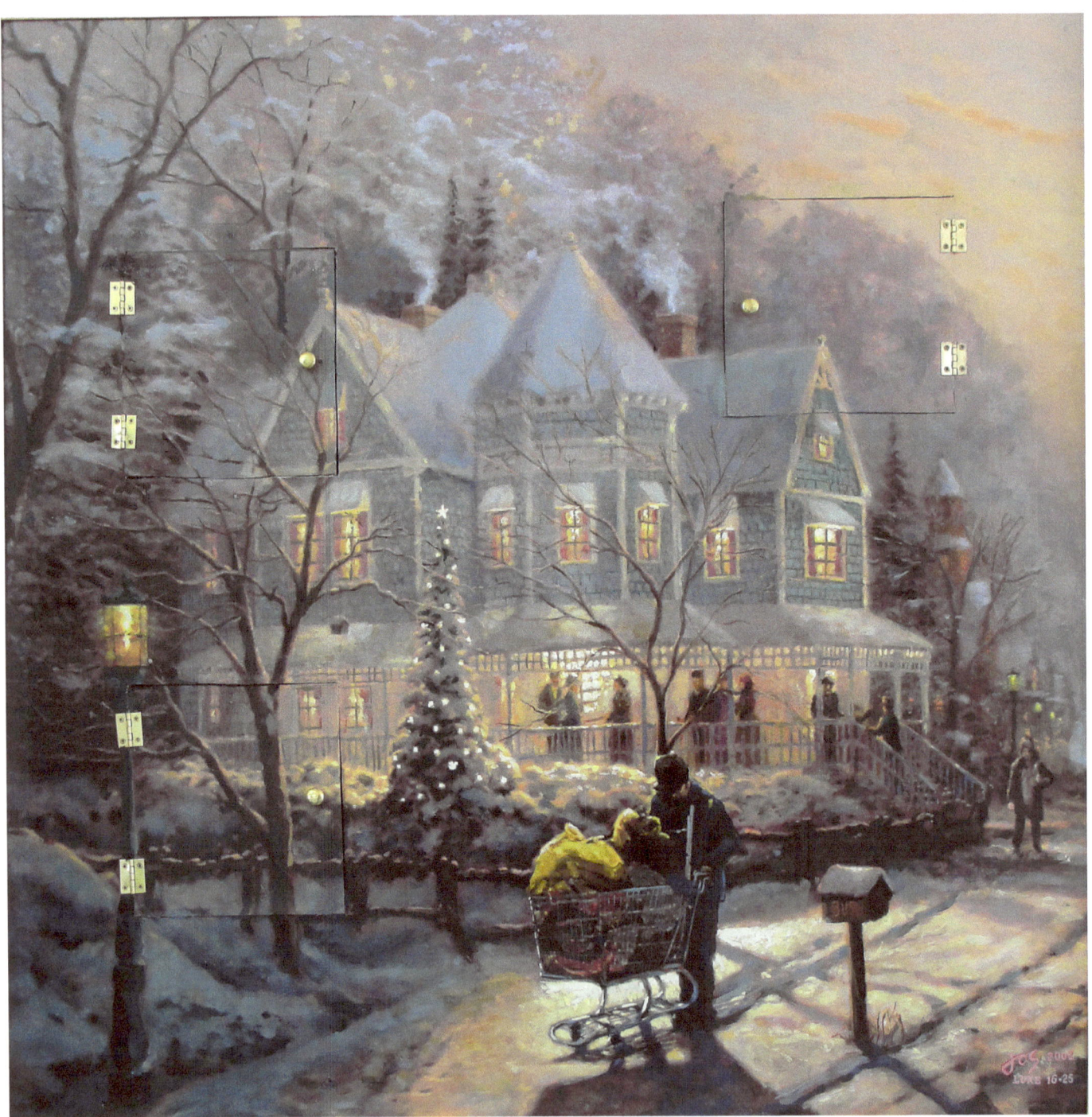

44

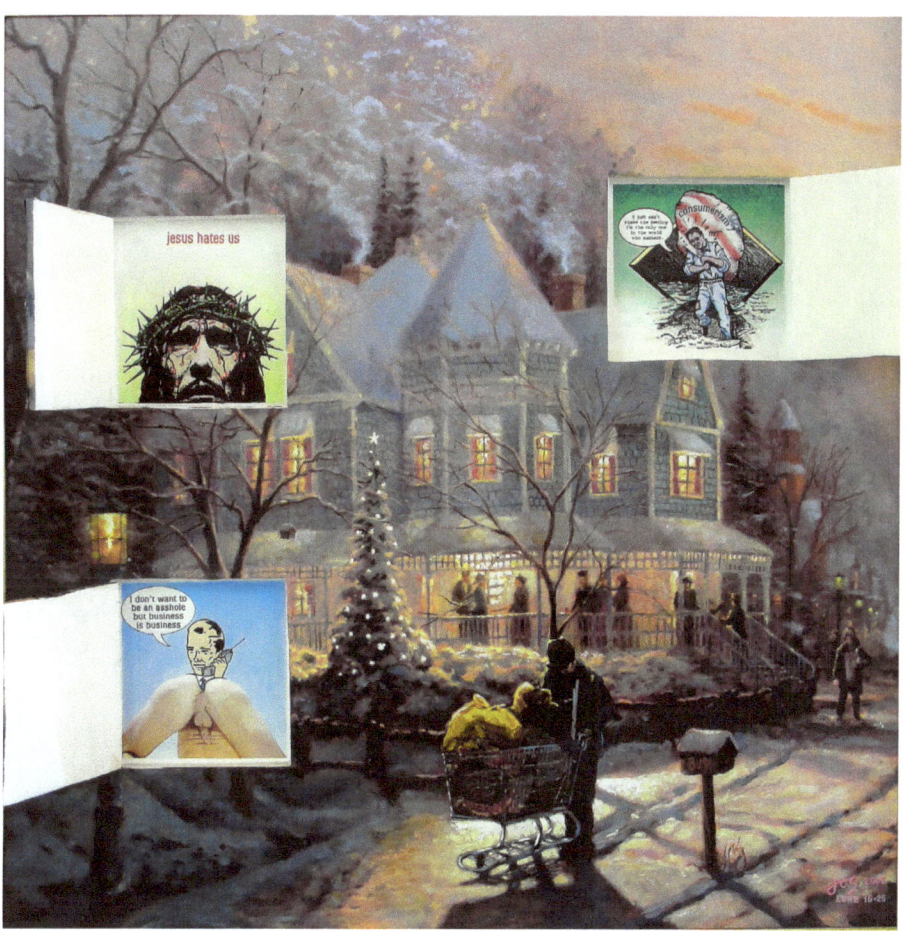

Figure 28 & 29.
Jos Sances
(1952-)
Holiday Home, 2002
Mixed Media Painting
33 x 33"
From the collection of Howard Levine
Reproduction Courtesy of the Artist

This reworking of a Thomas Kinkade painting of a romanticized Christmas celebration uses the sappy and nostalgic against itself. Hidden behind doors throughout the painting are further images that contrast the reality of American society with the saccharine dream of wealth. Behind the doors are commentaries on consumerism, religion and business. As is often the case in such pretty imagery there is a biblical quote. This one, altered from the original, is Luke 16:19-31 – the parable of the rich man who refused the poor man aid and burned in hell for eternity.

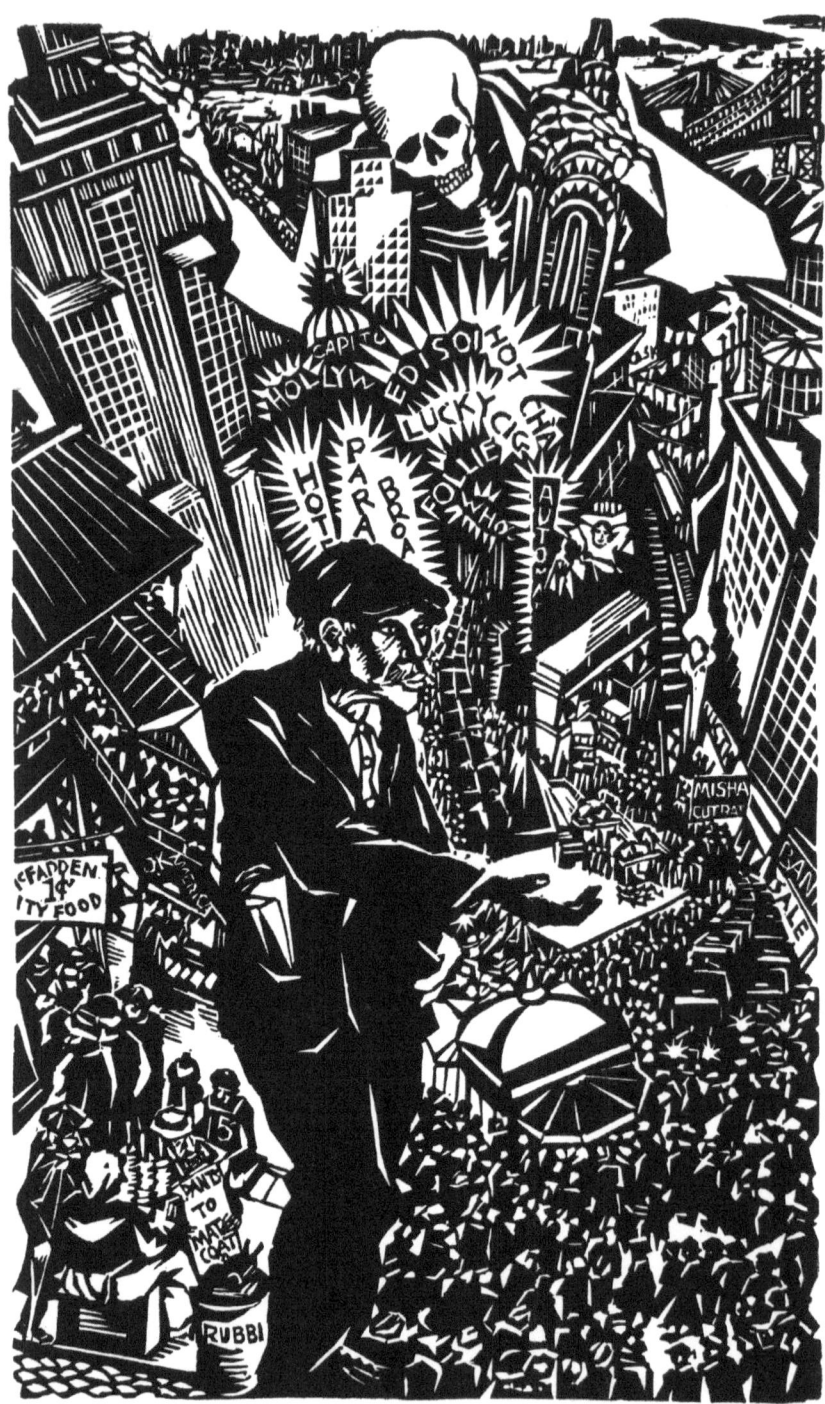

Figure 30.
Albert Potter
(1903–1937)
Brother Can You Spare A Dime, 1933/36
Woodcut, 13 x 8"
Reproduction with permission from the estate of Albert Potter and the Susan Teller Gallery
From the Collection of M. Lee Stone Fine Prints, San Jose, CA
Photo Credit: Robert Berger Photography

Potter lived most of his short life in New York and Rhode Island. From 1935 he was employed by the WPA/FAP. The title of this print, *Brother Can You Spare a Dime*, suggests Potter was probably thinking about the song of the same name that came out in 1931. The image disrupts the commonly held nostalgic view of the Depression as being a time when "we all pulled together." Clearly an era of haves and have-nots is portrayed both in this print and in the song that inspired it.

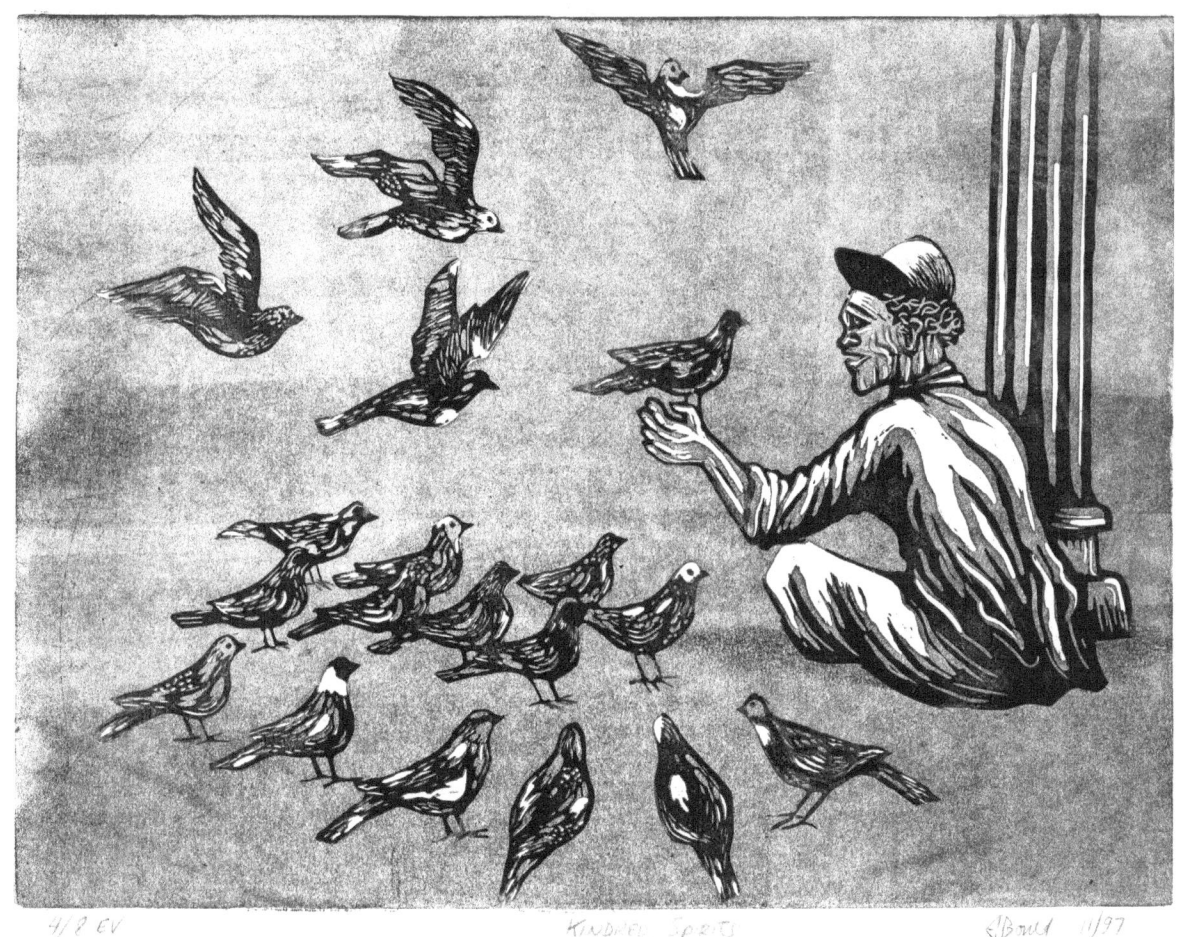

Gould has worked with several homeless rights groups, including the Coalition on Homelessness and the Homeless Advocacy Project, a group that helps people with legal assistance. He has also contributed to the *Street Sheet*. In this print, a moment of camaraderie with one of the most despised of urban animals, the pigeon, suggests a sense of well being but also a sense of alienation from society. The print might also bring to mind images of St. Francis talking with birds, especially knowing that it was made in San Francisco.

Figure 31
Ed Gould
(1932-)
Kindred Spirits, 1997
Woodcut, 8 3/4 x 11 3/4"
Reproduction Courtesy of the Artist

47

They used to tell me I was building a dream,
and so I followed the mob,
When there was earth to plow, or guns to bear,
I was always there right on the job.

They used to tell me I was building a dream,
with peace and glory ahead,
Why should I be standing in line,
just waiting for bread?

Once I built a railroad, I made it run,
made it race against time.
Once I built a railroad; now it's done.
Brother, can you spare a dime?

Figure 32.
Art Hazelwood
(1961-)
Four Freedoms, 1996
Linocut, 14 x 14"
Loaned for the exhibition by the Hearst
Art Gallery, Saint Mary's College of
California
Reproduction Courtesy of the Artist

In a 1941 speech, President Roosevelt outlined the "four essential human freedoms." They were then illustrated by Norman Rockwell in a famous series of paintings. Hazelwood, in a satirical twist, presents the reality of the basic freedoms for people in poverty. While Rockwell's painting showed Freedom from Want as a Thanksgiving dinner, this print portrays a woman with a sign asking for help. Next to her, the newspaper headline reads "Welfare Reform Planned," foreshadowing yet more draconian cuts to her livelihood. The notion that Welfare (AFDC, Aid for Families with Dependent Children) was the cause of homelessness rather than an attempt to alleviate poverty became a common belief in the 1980s.

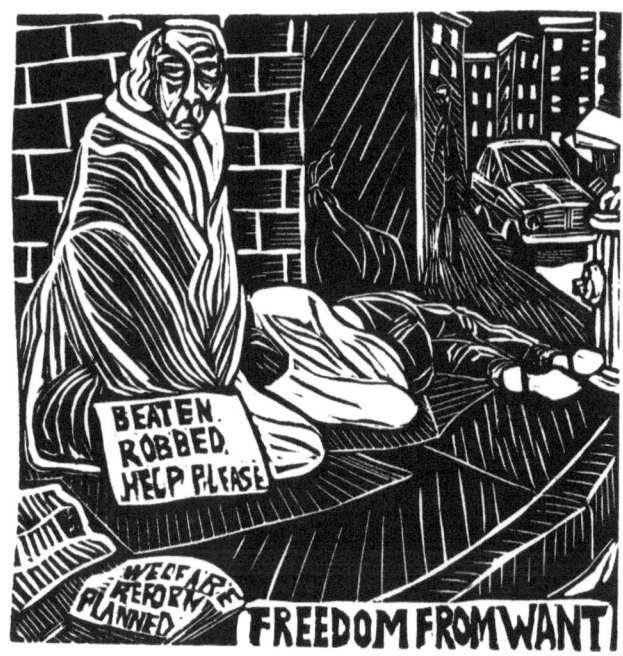

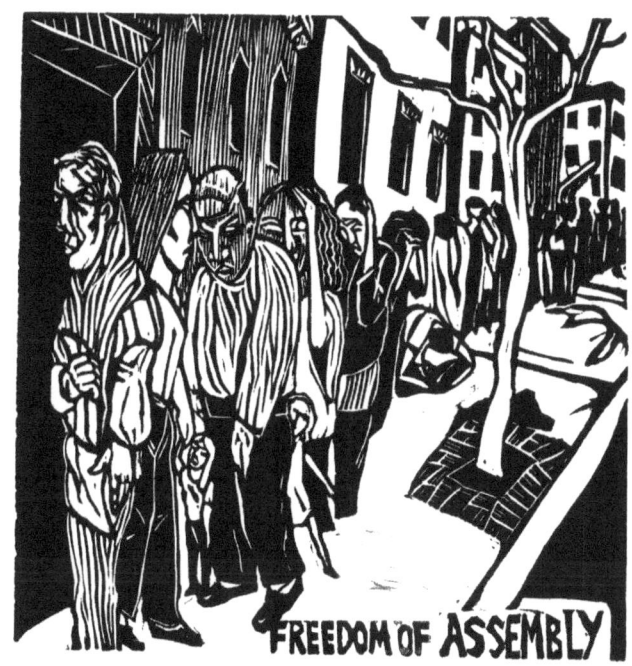

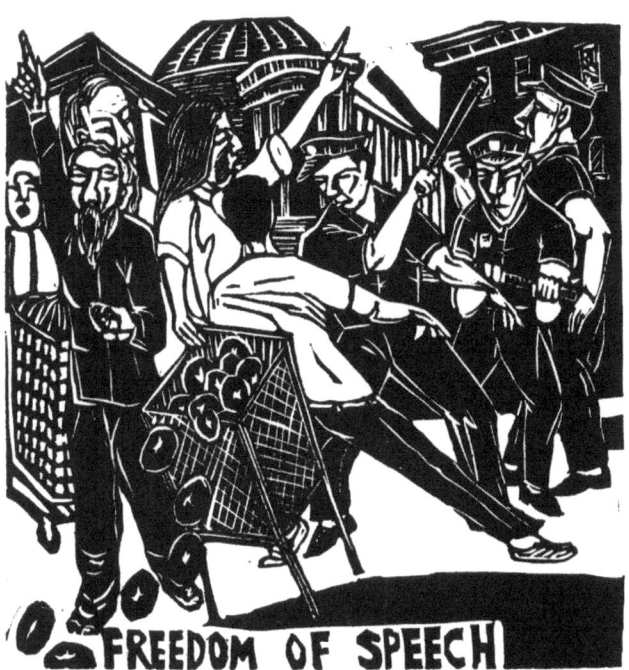

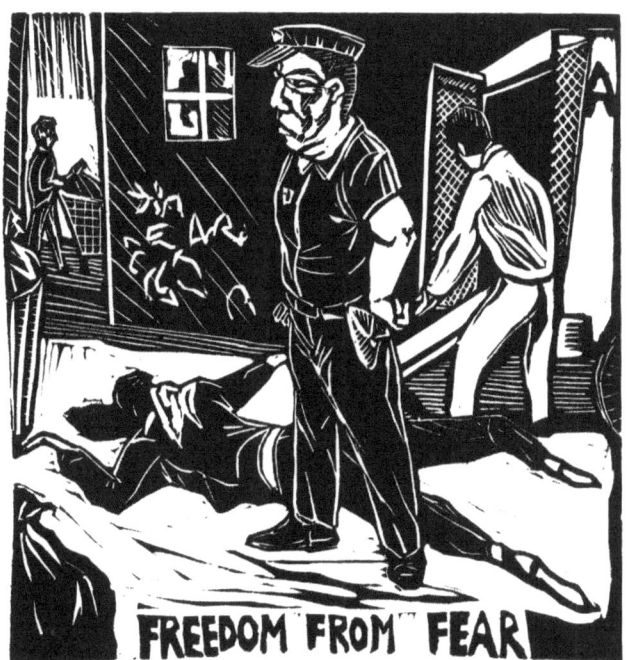

49

Displacement, Rootlessness and Vulnerability

During the Depression, signs were put up outside of towns warning people not to stop to look for work. Today, local laws close parks after dark, criminalize living on the street and urge "those people" to move on. Displaced workers, destitute children and families, drug addicts, veterans, immigrants, and the mentally ill wander from community to community seeking economic security, housing and health care. There is no stopping, no safe haven, no way back home. Tent cities spring up in the margins.

New Deal policies sought to create jobs in order to allow workers a way out of poverty. The link between labor struggles and battling poverty was a part of the philosophy of the New Deal and many artists saw the need to defend workers in their labor struggles. Today, artists have resumed portraying the consequences of economic and political forces that affect people's day-to-day lives.

The American rags to riches myth places the individual at the center of the story, pushing the community aside. For the heroic individual, this is the triumph over society. Yet when the individual falls—when industrial accident, displacement, or the mental and physical scars of war make the individual unable to work—then the inverse of the myth occurs. With no assistance from family or community, the dream of rising alone, turns into falling with no support.

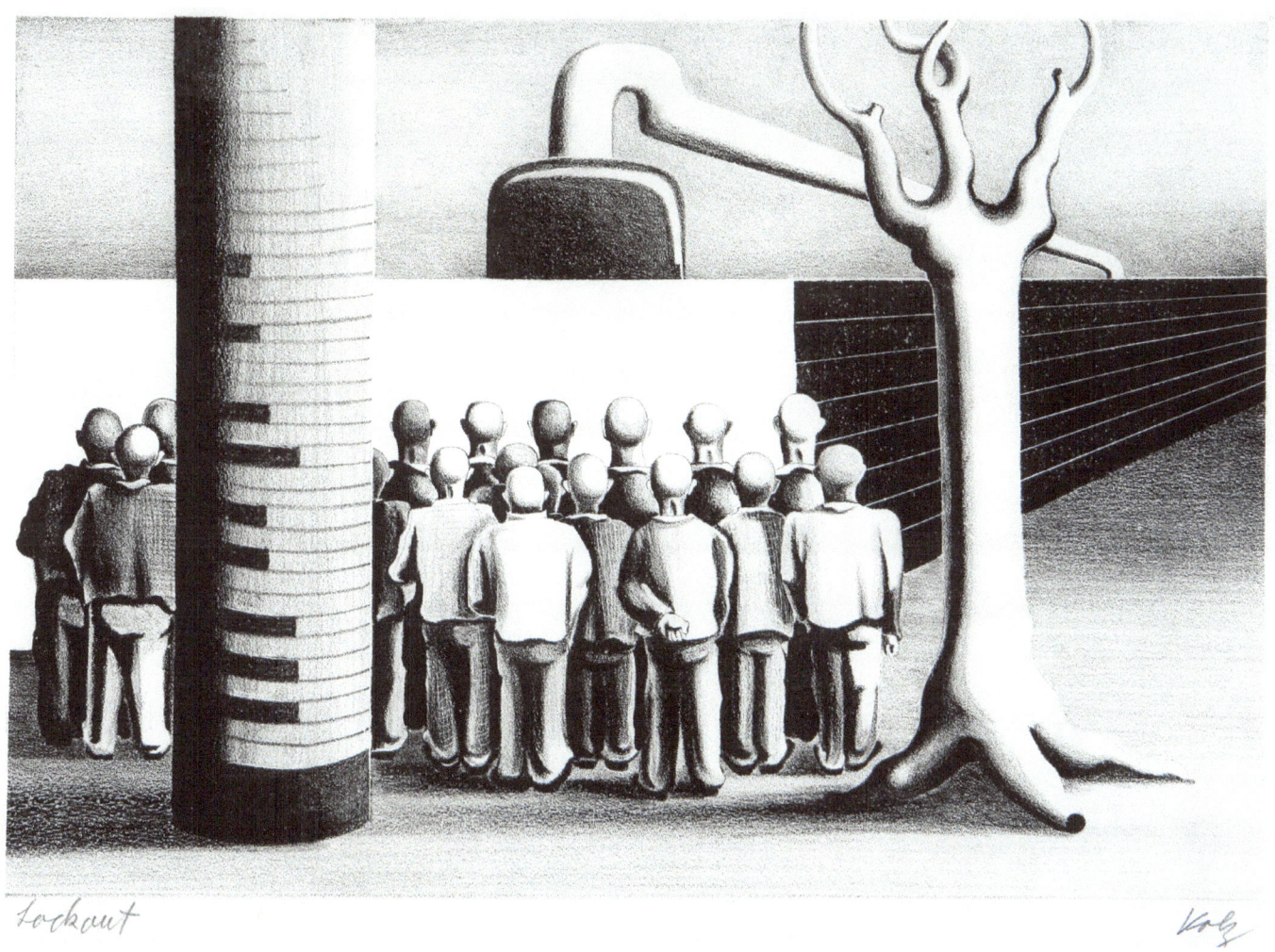

Lockout   *Volz*

In Lockout, Herman Volz depicts a lockout of factory workers—a tactic of employers to break the unity of workers during labor disputes. Born in Switzerland, Volz came to the United States in 1933. By 1937, he was working at the WPA/FAP lithographic section where he made this print. In 1938, he created what was considered at the time the largest mural in the world at the Golden Gate International Exposition on Treasure Island in San Francisco.

Figure 33.
Herman Volz
(1904-1990)
Lockout, c. 1938
Lithograph, 10 3/8 x 15 1/4"
Reproduction with permission from
Friedel Volz
Loaned for the exhibition by M. Lee
Stone Fine Prints, San Jose, CA
Photo Credit: Robert Berger Photography

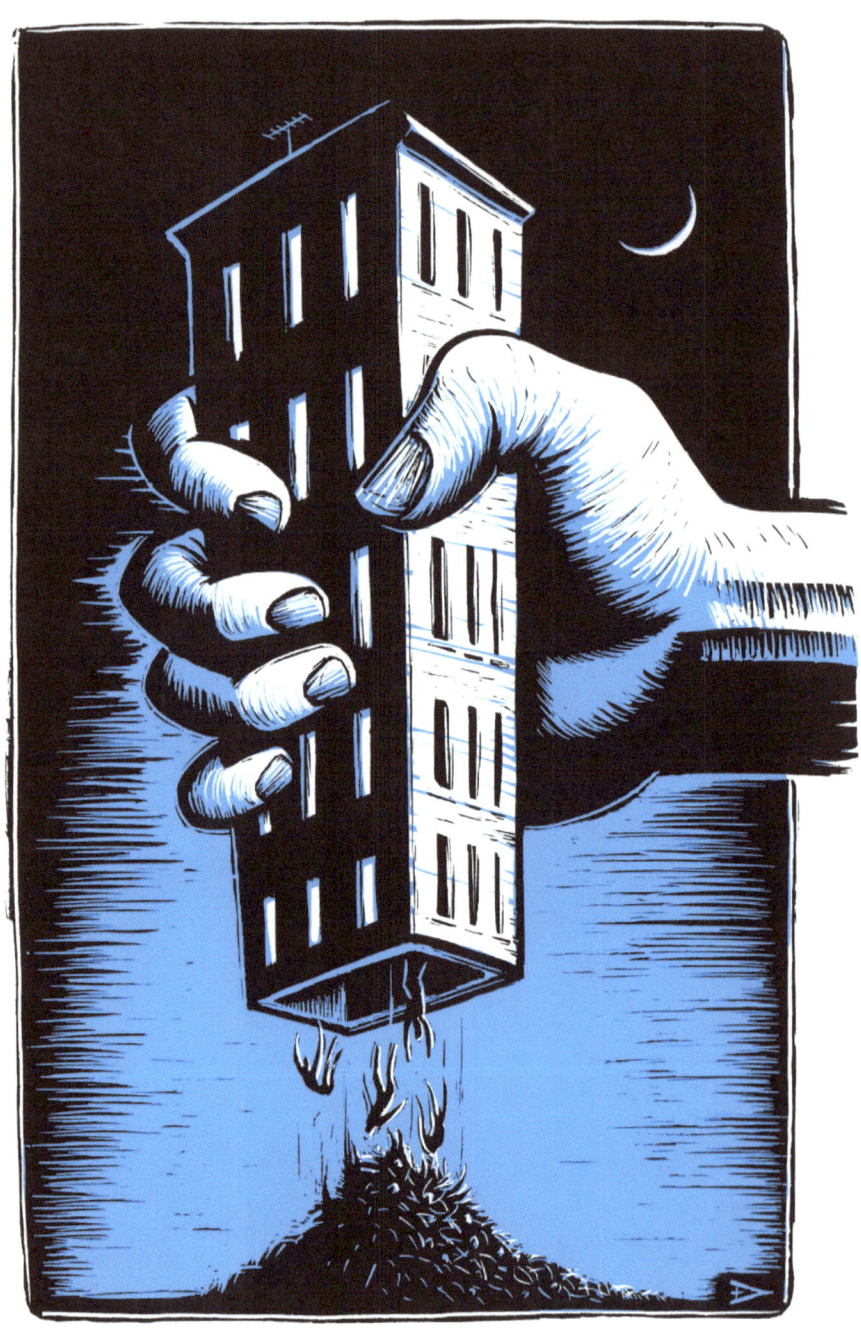

Figure 34.
Eric Drooker
(1958-)
The Hand That Takes, 1997
Digital Print of Original Scratch Board
Drawing, 17 x 11 1/2"
Reproduction Courtesy of the Artist

This image brings to mind Adam Smith's characterization of the "invisible hand" of the market, although in this version, the hand is a darker one than Smith imagined. Drooker shows the larger forces of the marketplace that have the power to displace at will. The image was originally created for publication in the *Village Voice* in 1997.

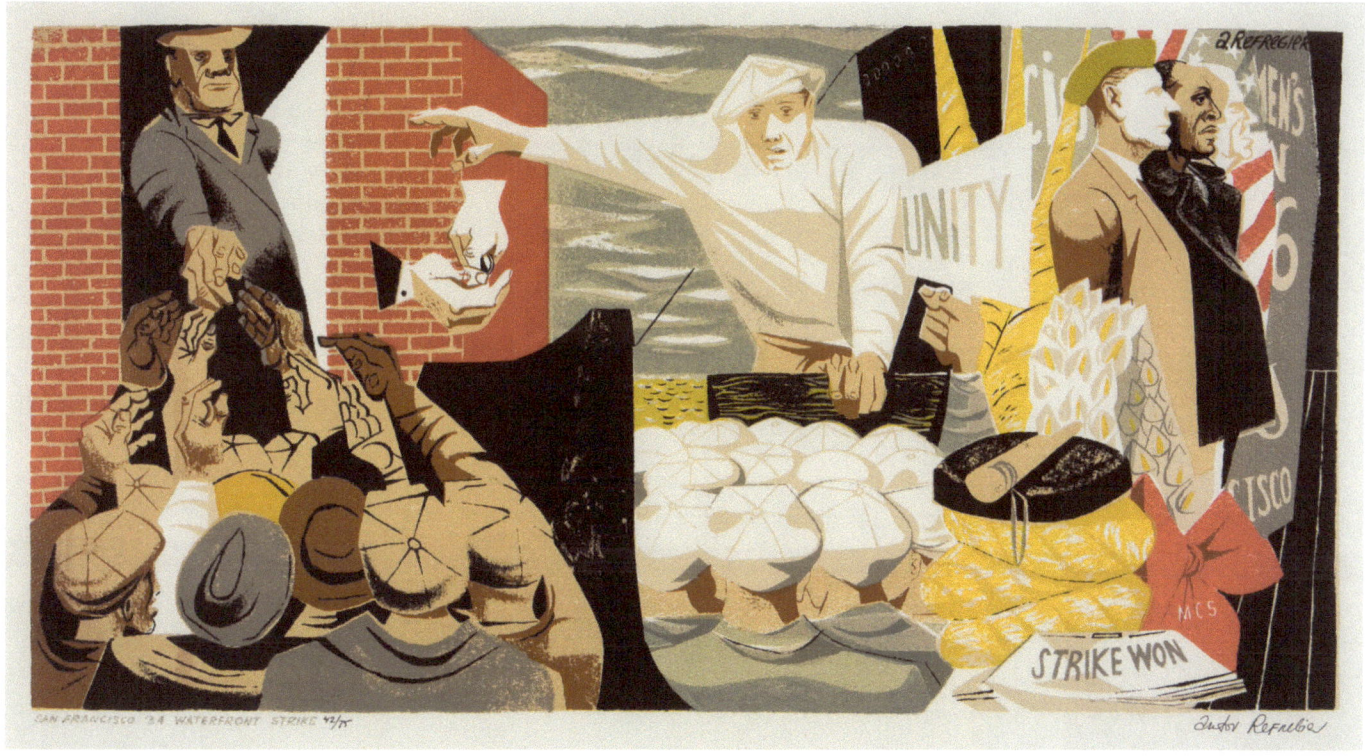

Figure 35.
Anton Refregier
(1905-1979)
San Francisco '34 Waterfront Strike, 1949
Screen Print, 11 1/4 x 22 1/4"
Reproduction with permission from
Brigit Refregier
From the Collection of M. Lee Stone Fine
Prints, San Jose, CA
Photo Credit: Robert Berger Photography

This print is based on a panel from Refregier's mural, "The History of California" at the Rincon Center in San Francisco. Refregier was forced to paint out parts to appease US government agencies and public opinion. After Republicans gained control of Congress and the Presidency in 1953, the murals became the focus of a Congressional investigation for anti-American content.[48]

'34 Waterfront Strike portrays events that led up to the General Strike of 1934. The left side shows a boss choosing workers for the day. The floating hands indicate that a bribe was demanded in order to secure work. The central figure is Harry Bridges, organizer of the International Longshoremen's and Warehousemen's Union (ILWU). He gestures toward the symbols of the corrupt system. Police and private security violence against striking dockworkers prompted a general strike of all workers of San Francisco. The wide support of the population of the city helped in the eventual victory of the Longshoreman in unionizing all the ports on the West Coast. The strike victory is represented on the right of the image.

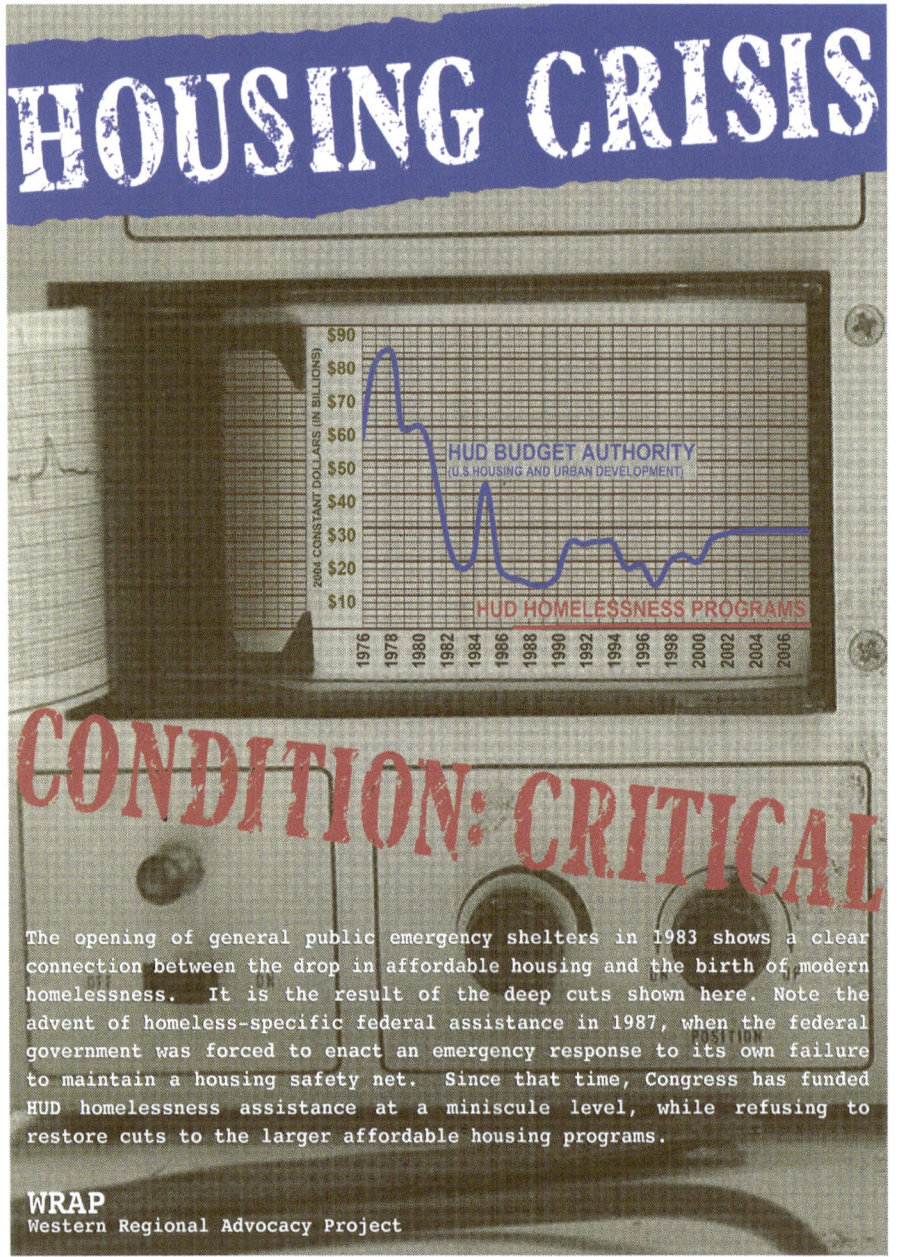

Figure 36.
Claude Moller
(1967-)
Housing Crisis, Condition: Critical, 2006
Screen Print, 22 x 16"
Reproduction Courtesy of the Artist
Loaned for the exhibition by Western
Regional Advocacy Project

This print was created for the Western Regional Advocacy Project (WRAP) for their report on federal spending priorities and homelessness. The statistical information on the image contrasts Department of Housing and Urban Development spending on new housing with all money for homeless assistance. Instead of subsidizing housing and addressing the root of homelessness (i.e. not enough affordable housing), the federal government is spending much less in the form of temporary assistance to homeless people.

Figure 37.
Doug Minkler
(1949-)
Who Drives the Cycle of Poverty?, 1997
Screen Print, 20 x 26"
Reproduction Courtesy of the Artist

Doug Minkler has created political posters for more than three decades and sells them on the street every weekend on bustling Telegraph Avenue, a couple of blocks south of UC Berkeley. He considers it his role as an artist to help social justice organizations with fund raising, outreach and education. He has worked with Rain Forest Action Network, ACLU, Veteran's for Peace and many other groups.

"Cycle of poverty" is a term that suggests the endless inability of poor people to get out of poverty. In this poster for the National Lawyers Guild's Campaign for Economic Justice, Minkler turns the expression on its head by humorously begging the question, who drives this cycle? Using his art as a means to educate, Minkler explicitly cites many of the true culprits perpetuating poverty.

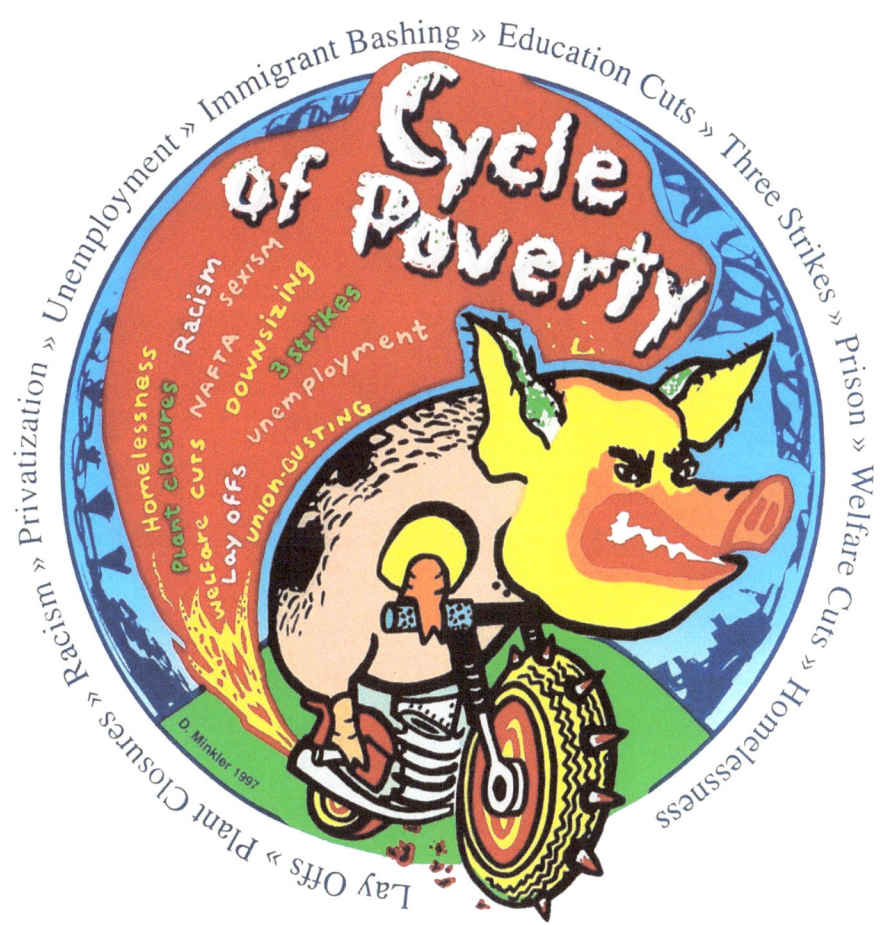

Who Drives the Cycle of Poverty?

A. Welfare Queens   **B.** Illegal Aliens
C. Bleeding Heart Liberals   D. Capitalist Pigs

Crash the Cycle of Poverty!
Join the National Lawyers Guild's
Campaign For Economic Justice

Answer: D.

55

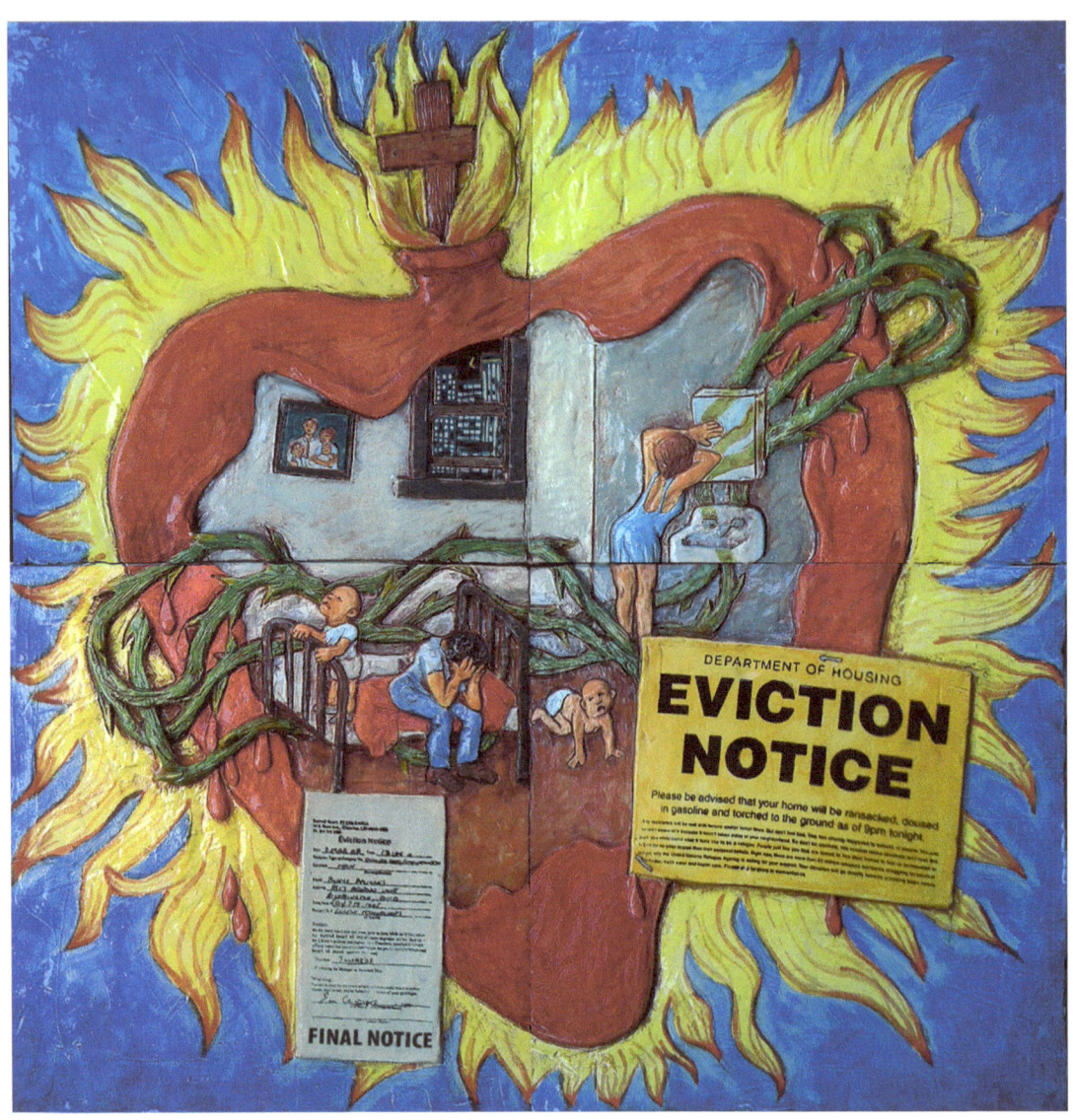

Figure 38.
Jos Sances
(1952-)
Sacred Heart, 2008
Ceramic Tile, 24 x 24"
Reproduction Courtesy of the Artist

Sances has a long history as a screenprint poster artist. In 1980, he co-founded Mission Gráfica, a community screenprint workshop in San Francisco's Mission District that played a central role in the Latino Art Movement. He founded the union screenprint and design shop Alliance Graphics in 1989. He is also a muralist and ceramicist. The sacred heart, a Catholic symbol of the suffering and comfort of Jesus, is here portrayed as a record of the suffering of those who have been evicted.

Figure 39.
Sandow Birk
(1962-)
GI Homecoming, 2008
Oil on Canvas, 30 x 24"
Reproduction Courtesy of the Artist
Loaned for the exhibition by Catharine
Clark Gallery, San Francisco

Sandow Birk has based his painting
on Norman Rockwell's 1945 painting
titled *Homecoming GI.* In the original,
an enthusiastic family bursts with
open arms from tenement housing,
everyone rises to greet the returning vet. In Birk's version, the housing
complex is a place of little hope and
less enthusiasm, and the lost limbs
of the soldier testify to a bleak future.
Birk moves the setting from an East
Coast tenement apartment to Jordan
Downs, one of the main public housing projects in Los Angeles.

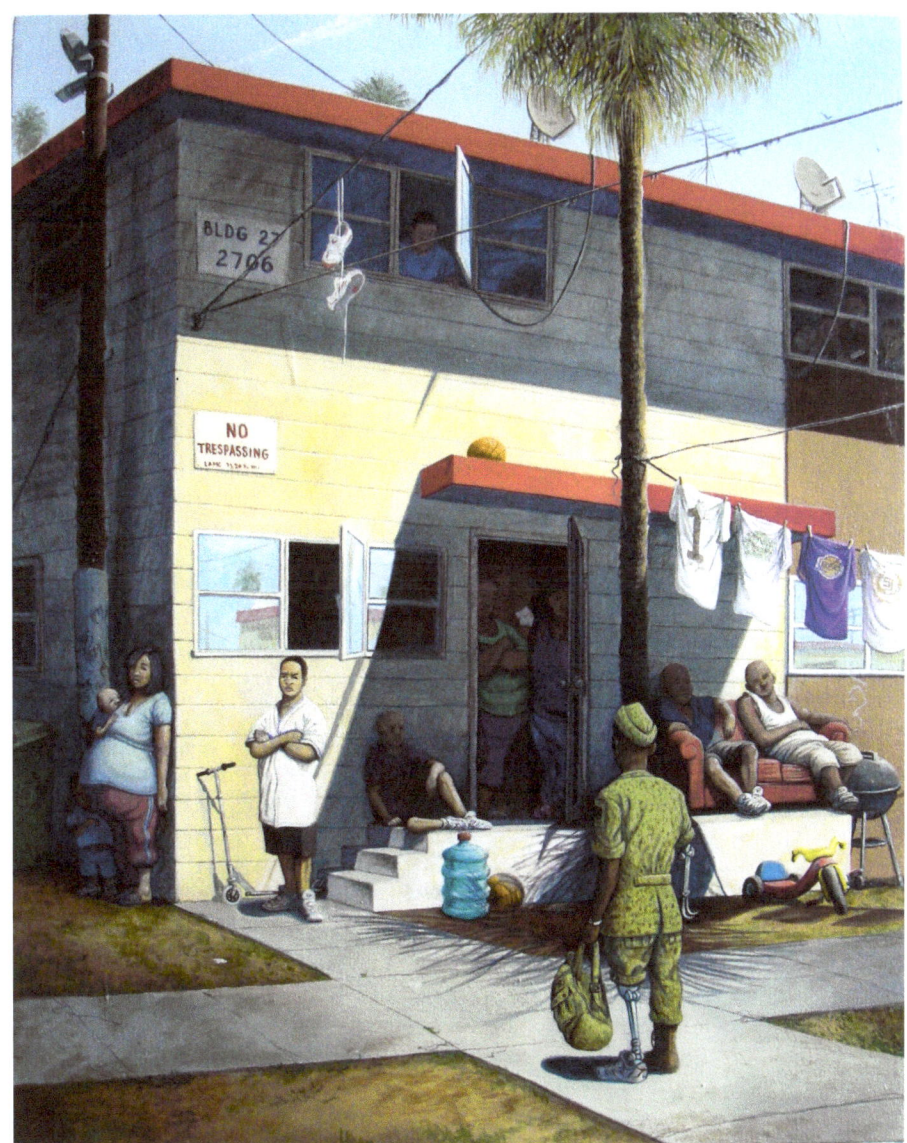

Figure 40.
Dorothea Lange
(1895-1965)
Migrants, family of Mexicans, on road with tire trouble. Looking for work in the peas. California. 1936/1975
Library of Congress photograph on Agfa Portriga paper, 11 x 14"
Reproduction Courtesy of the Prints and Photographs Division, Library of Congress, Washington, D.C.
Collection of de Saisset Museum, Santa Clara University, NDA.6.589
Photo Credit: Robert Berger Photography

Lange documented the plight of the rural migrants from the Dust Bowl states of the lower Midwest who poured into California. But she also documented the Mexican farm workers who had been in California before the Depression but were largely forced out by tighter visa regulations during the Depression. As World War II created greater demand for farm labor, Mexican workers returned under the 1942 Bracero program, a guest worker program that offered little in the way of rights to the workers.

On the Move: Urban Vs. Rural

Homelessness takes many forms. While for many people homelessness is symbolized by someone pushing a shopping cart, it is not representative of most forms of homelessness.

In rural settings, homelessness often means living in a shanty or a car. Images of cardboard shacks built by agricultural workers reflect the fact that work alone does not guarantee adequate housing.

In urban areas homeless people are grouped together around service providers and kept out of prosperous neighborhoods. They remain on the move because of laws against camping, sitting, lying, panhandling, sleeping, blocking the sidewalk, and possessing "stolen property" (i.e. shopping carts and milk crates.)

While homeless people disappear from "view" into rural vastness or urban pockets of poverty, artists have worked to make homelessness visible. Documentation of living conditions creates a powerful voice of moral outrage.

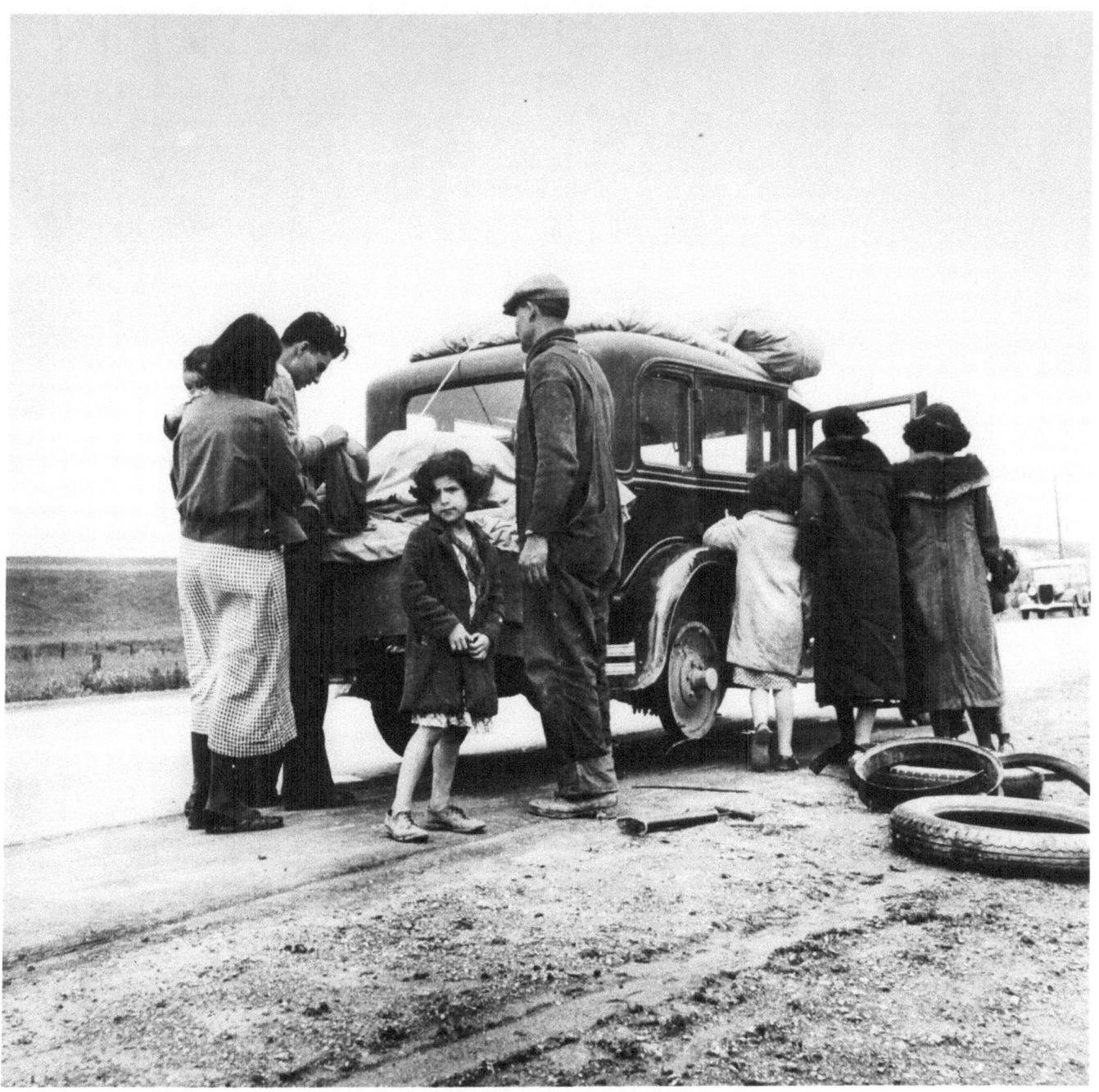

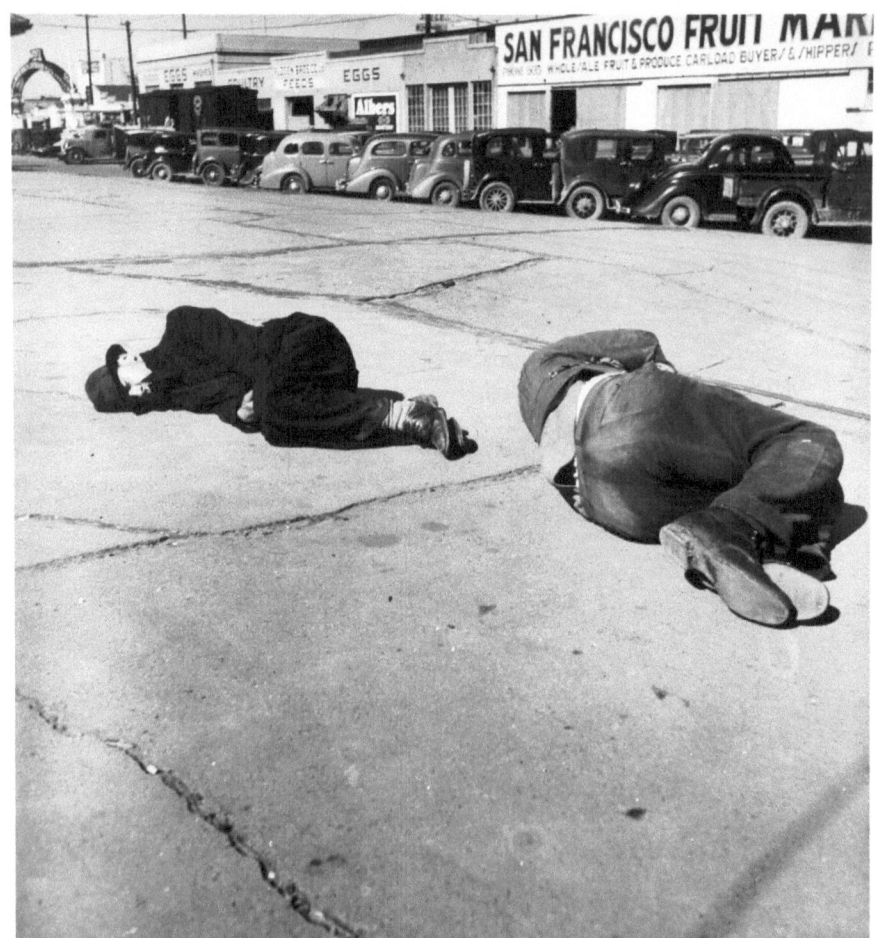

Figure 41.
Dorothea Lange
(1895-1965)
Scene along "Skid Row," Howard Street, San Francisco, California, 1937
Library of Congress photograph on Agfa Portriga paper, 14 x 11"
Reproduction Courtesy of the Prints and Photographs Division, Library of Congress, Washington, D.C.
Collection of de Saisset Museum, Santa Clara University, NDA.6.592
Photo Credit: Robert Berger Photography

Although Lange's images often portray rural conditions, most homeless people during the Depression years gathered in urban areas. In the early 1930s Lange's interest in social issues grew, and she began to photograph unemployed and destitute people. A 1934 exhibition of her photographs drew the attention of Paul Taylor, an activist economics professor at UC Berkeley who hired Lange to document and photograph elements of his reports on rural poverty in California. This work led her to the federal Resettlement Administration in 1935 to photograph conditions of rural poverty.

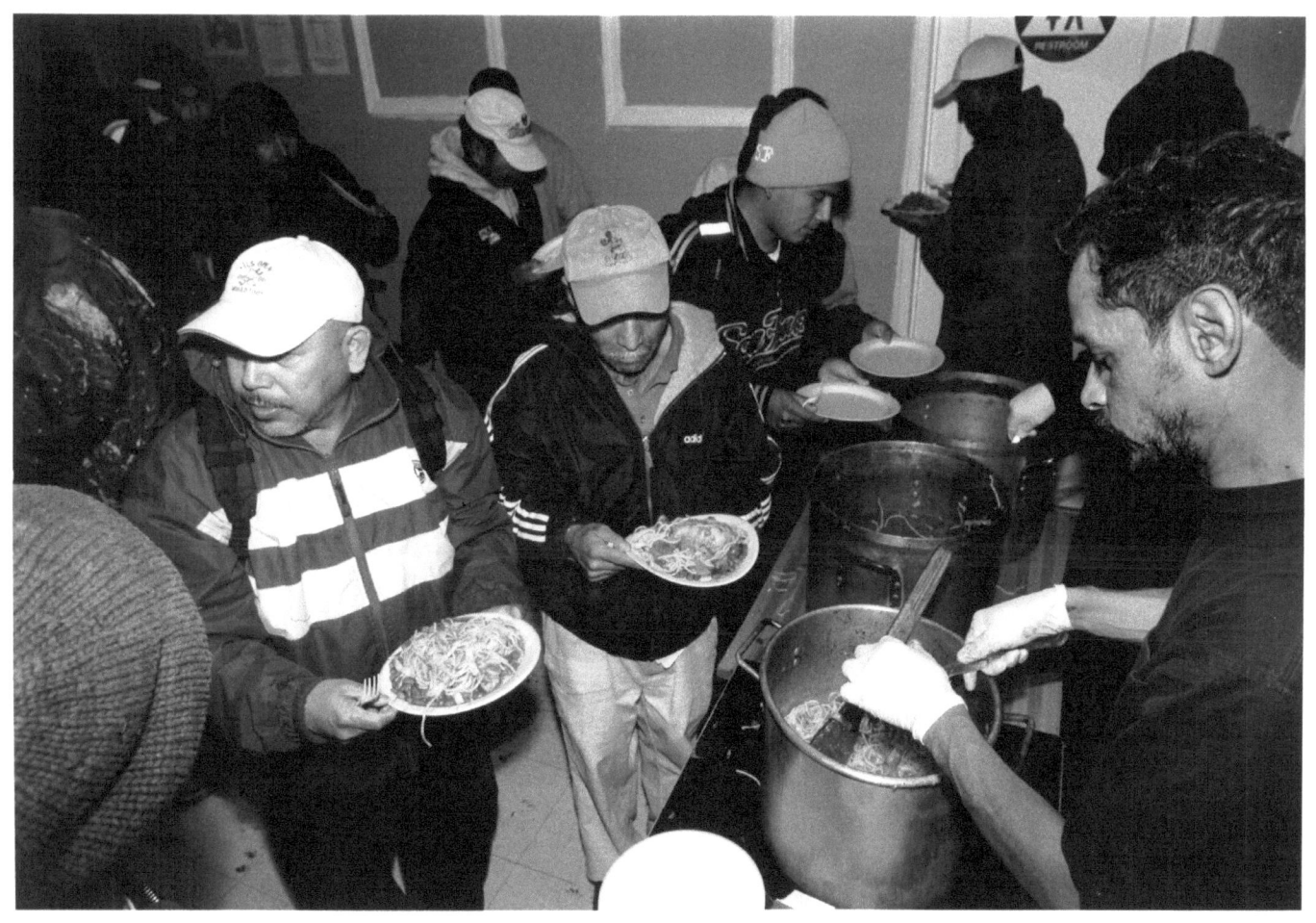

Economic conditions in Latin America displace workers who then move north in large numbers. When they arrive in the US, these workers often find themselves in conditions of virtual servitude. The "Day Laborer Soup Kitchen" presents an urban side of contemporary poverty. Day labor centers provide food to those workers whose temporary employment leaves them vulnerable to sudden loss of income. Migrants from Mexico and Central America made up the majority of the regulars at this center in San Francisco.

Figure 42.
Francisco Dominguez
(1959-)
Day Laborer Soup Kitchen, 2008
Silver Gelatin Print, 12 x 18"
Reproduction Courtesy of the Artist

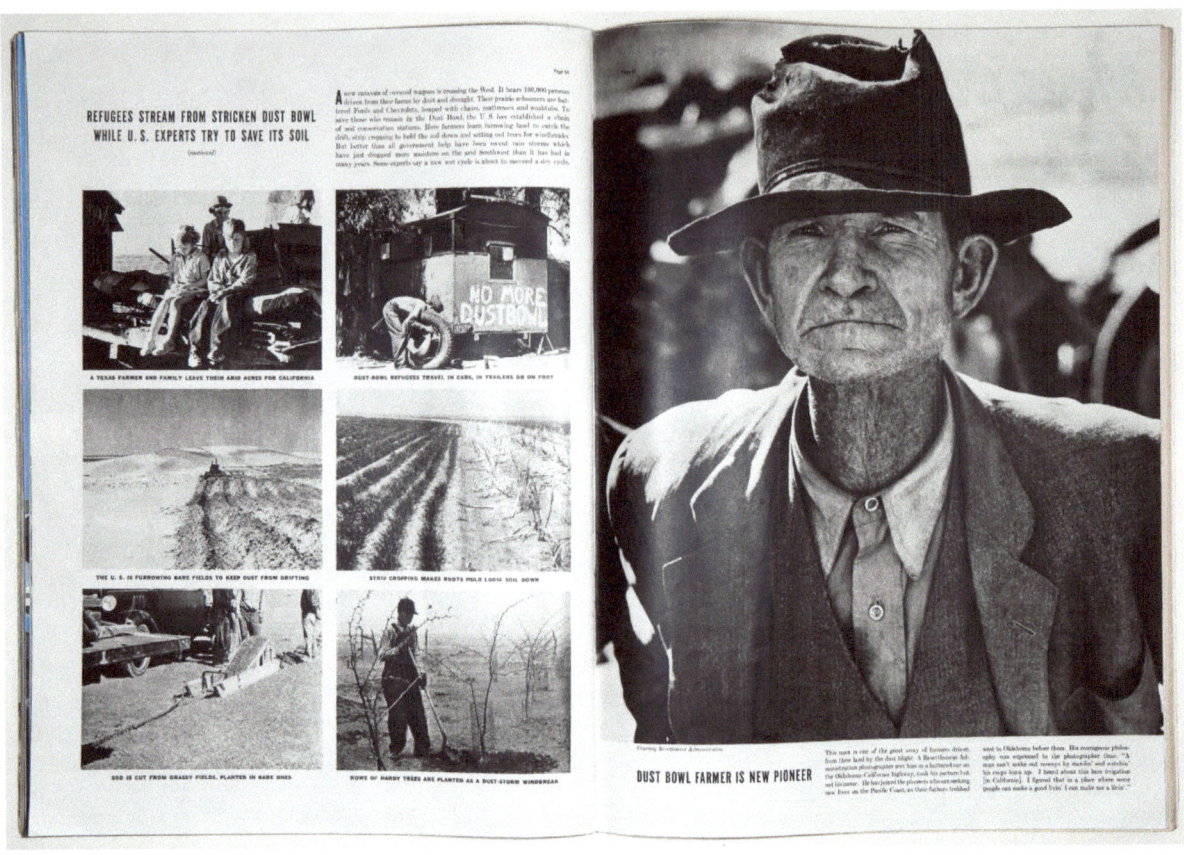

Lange's photographs were intended to support the establishment of migrant camps by the Resettlement Administration, later the FSA. Between 1937 and 1940 Lange's photos were used as congressional testimony to the US Senate, for WPA exhibits, and by a number of newspapers and periodicals.

Both the FSA's Roy Stryker and Dorothea Lange were eager to place a story about migrant workers in popular *Life* magazine. Yet of all the images submitted, only one of Lange's photographs ever appeared. Concluding a six-page spread on the Dust Bowl that optimistically highlighted new farming practices, the magazine displayed a striking full-page close-up of a man with a defiant glance. Lange was not credited, although the FSA was. The caption, "Dust Bowl Farmer is New Pioneer," was deceptive but the image still communicates great power.

Figure 43.
LIFE Magazine
June 21, 1937, 14 x 10 1/2"

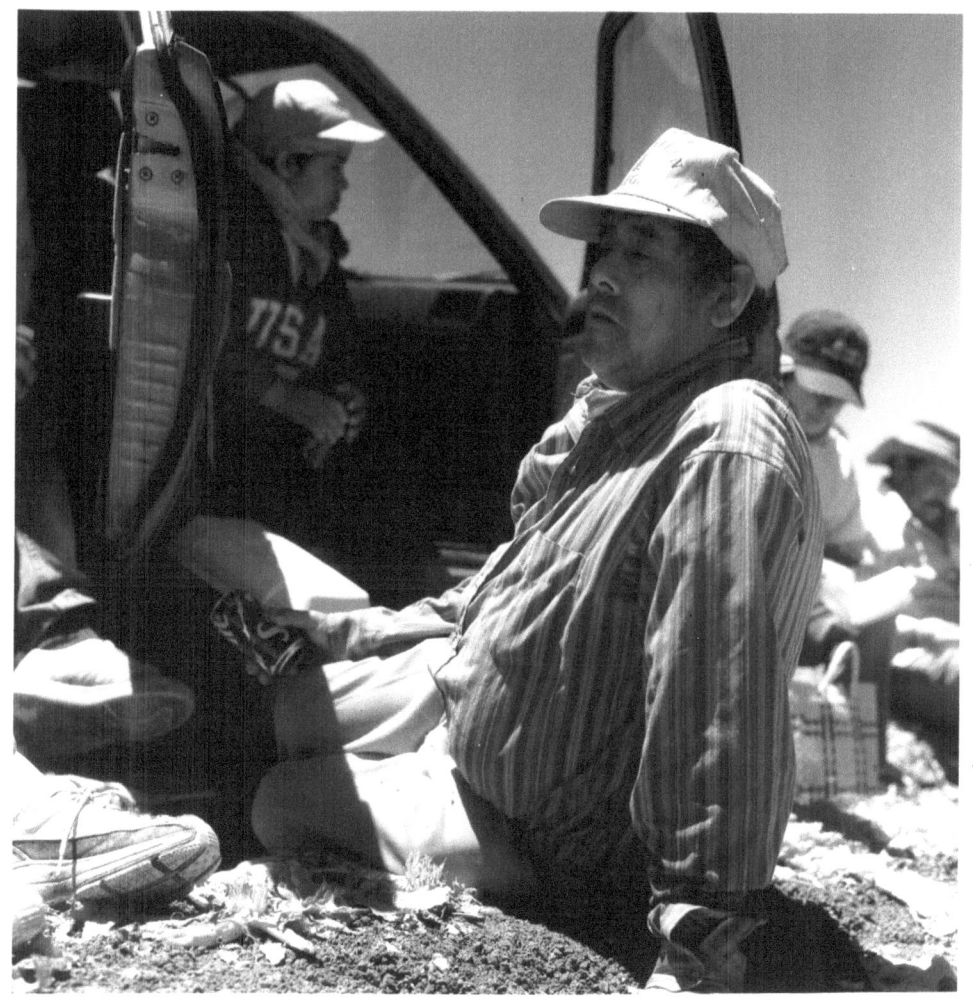

Migrant workers in this photograph sleep under bridges, in ditches or in vehicles and follow the crops throughout the upper Sacramento Valley. The farther one goes into rural areas, the less government oversight there is of living conditions of migrant workers. In 2005, an estimated 7.8 million people in rural areas lived in poverty (14.6% of the total rural population).[49]

Francisco Dominguez's interest in the lives and conditions of farm workers and immigrants derives from his own family legacy as agricultural workers. His father was a Bracero worker who earned his US citizenship by signing up to fight in the Korean War. His mother worked the fields sorting tomatoes in the Sacramento Valley.

Figure 44.
Francisco Dominguez
(1959-)
Colusa County, Migrant workers taking a break from picking squash, 2003
Silver Gelatin Print, 14 x 14"
Reproduction Courtesy of the Artist

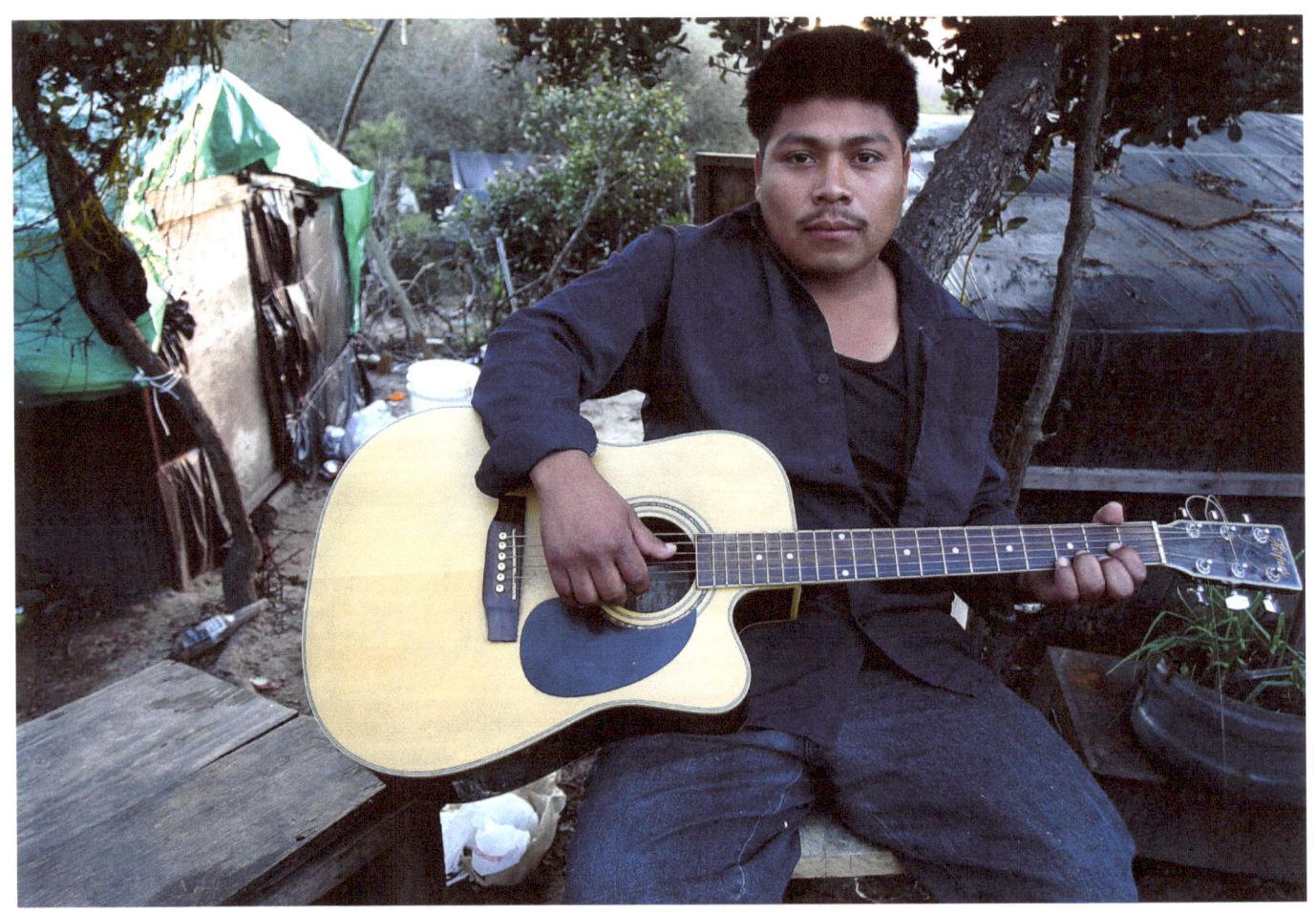

Figure 45.
David Bacon
(1948-)
San Diego, A young Mixtec man with the guitar he brought with him from Oaxaca, playing the music of his home village, 2005
Photograph, 16 x24"
Reproduction Courtesy of the Artist

David Bacon is both a writer and photographer. He has written about the effects of globalization and the criminalization of immigrants. Akin to the ideals of the 1930s, his photographs capture the human dignity of his subjects. He also reveals inhumane living conditions, as in this photo of an agricultural worker in San Diego county. These conditions are not unique to San Diego County. As a former organizer for the United Farm Workers, Bacon observes that many workers today are living in conditions much worse than any seen in the last forty years.

After this series of photographs was taken, the vigilante group calling themselves Minute Men chased the workers out of this encampment.[50] The Depression saw similar vigilante groups attacking Dust Bowl migrants

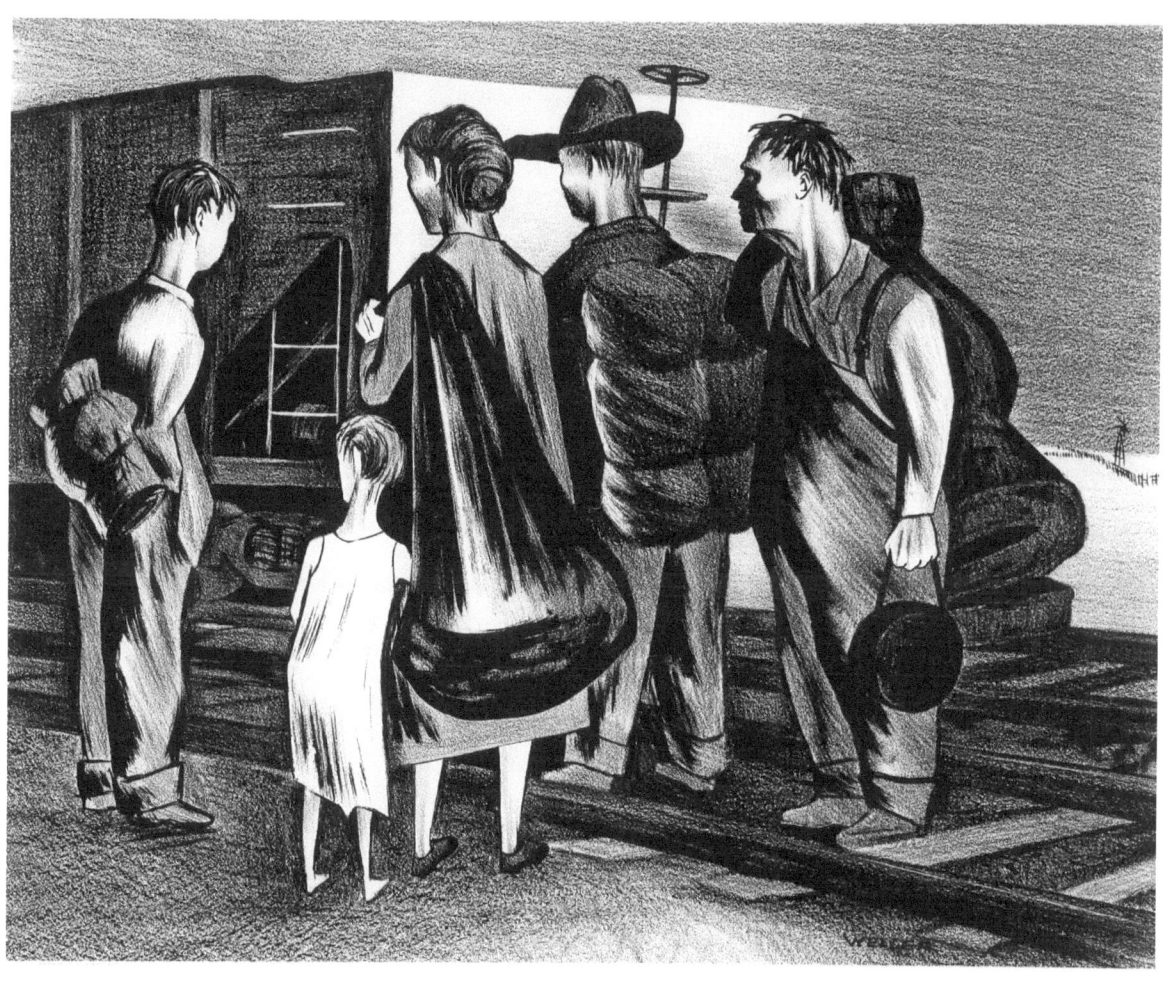

In 1930, at the age of eighteen, Weller hopped a freight train and traveled through the West. He worked on ranches and on Boulder Dam, a massive New Deal construction project that attracted workers from all over the country. The memory of the trains he rode, and the hobos and migrant people he met during these years are often represented in his work.

Riding the rails, which since the 19th century had served as a dependable means for the movement of poor people to find work, was made increasingly difficult in the Post War era by tighter security in the rail yards.

Figure 46.
Paul Weller
(1912-2000)
Harvest Hands, 1937
Lithograph, 11 1/2 x 14 1/2"
Reproduction Courtesy of the Estate of
Paul Weller
From the Collection of M. Lee Stone Fine
Prints, Inc., San Jose, CA
Photo Credit: Robert Berger Photography

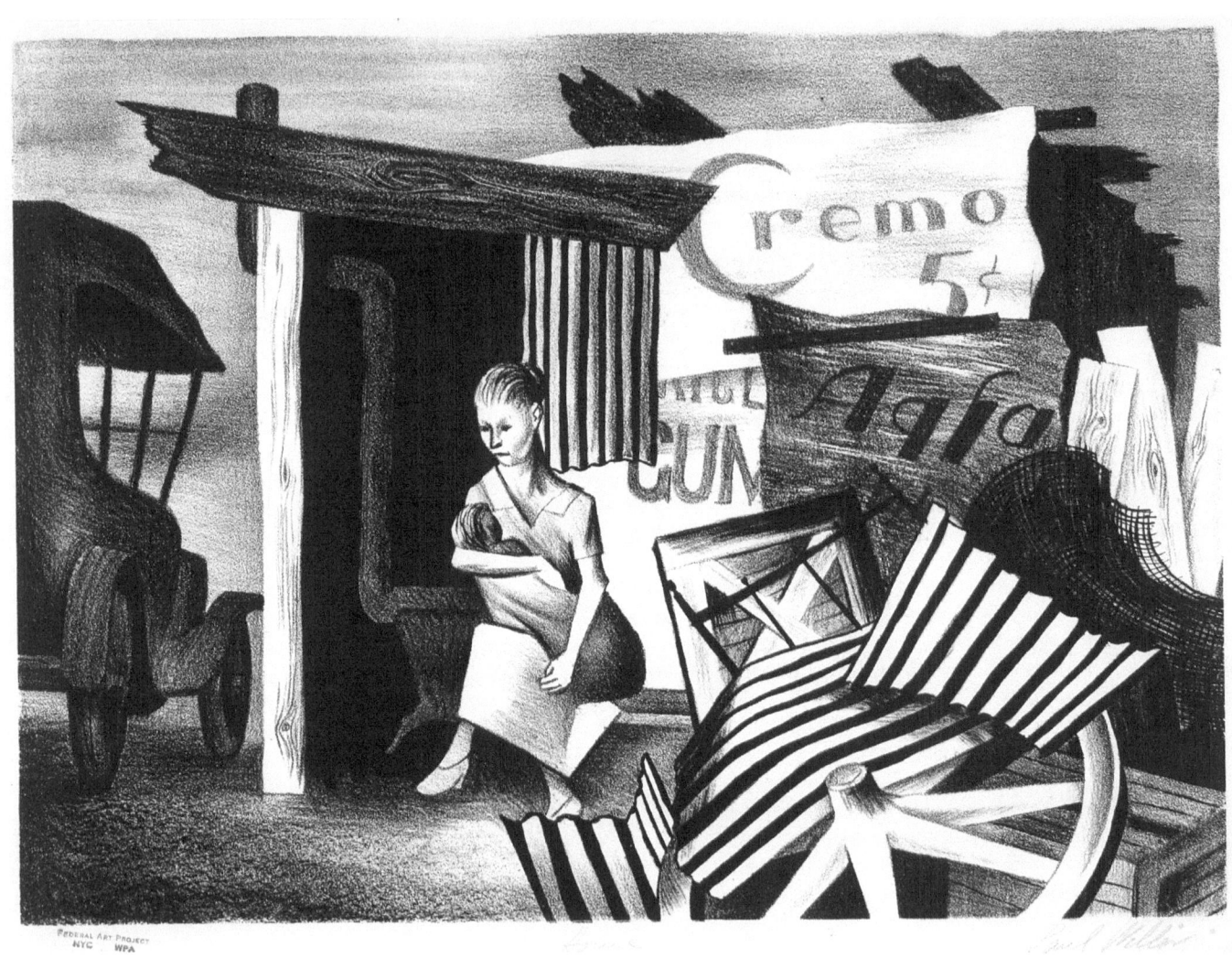

Figure 47.
Paul Weller
(1912-2000)
Home, c. 1937
Lithograph, 10 1/2 x 14 1/2"
Reproduction Courtesy of Estate
of Paul Weller
From the Collection of M. Lee Stone Fine
Prints, Inc., San Jose, CA
Photo Credit: Robert Berger Photography

Several years of tramping through the Western states and Weller's own experiences as a migrant worker acquainted him with poor housing conditions as represented in this print. In the late 1930s he turned these memories into lithographic prints after he arrived in New York City and began working for the WPA/FAP in the graphics division

66

Struggle & Hope

"Then I'll be around in the dark.. I'll be ever'where—wherever you look. Wherever they's a fight so hungry people can eat. I'll be there. Wherever they's a cop beatin' up a guy, I'll be there. An' when our folks eat the stuff they raise an' live in the houses they build—why, I'll be there. See?"[51]

Tom Joad
John Steinbeck, The Grapes of Wrath, 1939

The struggles and hopes of homeless people have changed as views of government's role in society have changed. During the Great Depression, many unemployed families lived in Hoovervilles. The government responded with programs to put people to work and provide basic housing. The success of these programs can be seen in the buildings, dams, bridges and artwork created by the New Deal, as well as in the legacy of government programs such as Social Security that created an economic safety net for Americans.

By the late 1970s, the view of government's role had shifted so that social programs were redefined as a burden on the American taxpayer rather than a hard-won social benefit. In this era, artists again began to take a more adversarial role in challenging government and society's indifference. Artists allied themselves with activists and worked to encourage society to recognize the need to offer protection from the whims of fate and an unjust social system.

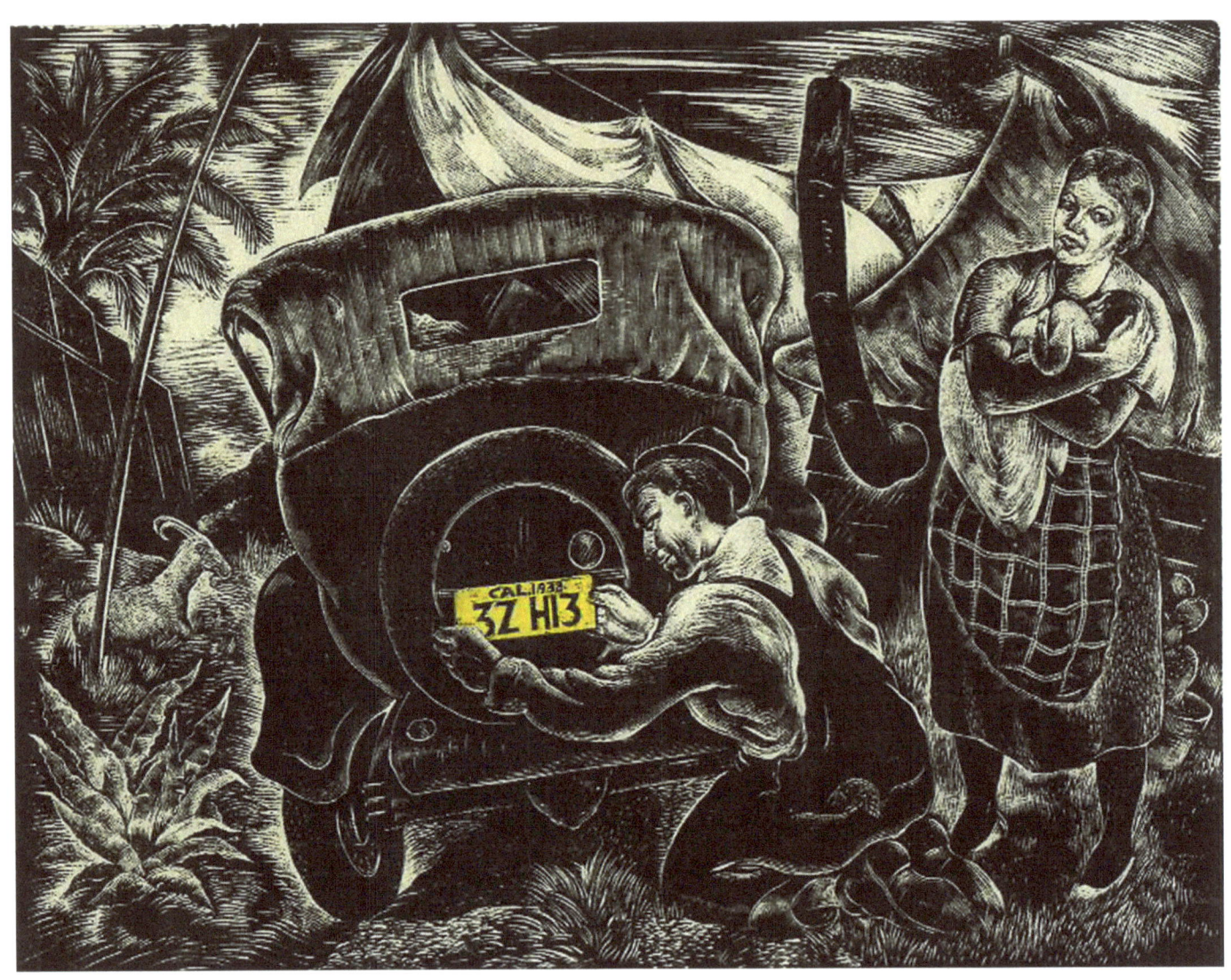

Figure 48.
Charles Surendorf
(1906-1979)
California, 1938
Wood Engraving, 6 x 8"
Courtesy of Surendorf Gallery Collection

Born in Indiana, Charles Surendorf moved to California in 1929. The artist's own experience with migration to California perhaps gave him some insight into the pride expressed by the father as he attaches a California license plate to the family car. The plate's gold color—the only color in the print—underscores the hope of "golden opportunity." The mother's expression, however, is more ambiguous. Perhaps it hints at resignation to the need for protection from anti-migrant forces that might see those with an out-of-state license plate as a family to attack.

One episode illustrates some of the fear that immigrants to California might have felt. In 1936, the Los Angeles Police Department sent 136 officers to 16 major points along the Arizona, Nevada and Oregon state lines, with orders to turn back migrants. The so called "Bum Blockade" offered those stopped a choice of turning around and leaving the state or facing 180 days in jail.[52] In 1937, California then passed a law making it a misdemeanor to assist an indigent person in coming to California.[53] These "Anti-Okie Laws" were not the only thing to fear. Vigilante groups commonly were reported to harass migrants. By 2010, attacks on immigrants and homeless people were continuing to rise nationwide, with assaults, rapes, and murders all increasing. Even setting homeless people on fire is no longer an isolated occurrence.[54]

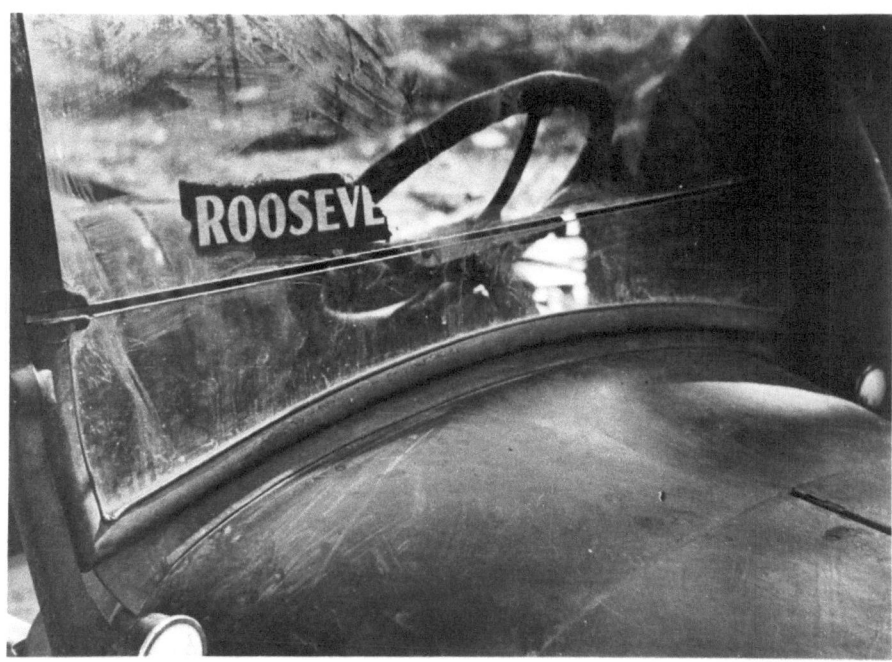

Figure 49.
Dorothea Lange
(1895-1965)
The windshield of a migratory agricultural laborer's car, in a squatter camp near Sacramento, California, 1936
Library of Congress photograph on Agfa Portriga paper, 11 x 14"
Reproduction Courtesy of the Prints and Photographs Division, Library of Congress, Washington, D.C.
Collection of de Saisset Museum, Santa Clara University, NDA.6.594
Photo Credit: Robert Berger Photography

Hope and the fading of hope are expressed in the bumper sticker on this migratory worker's car. While Franklin Roosevelt's administration had achieved much in its first term, large numbers of people remained plagued by terrible poverty. Roosevelt spoke openly of the shortcomings of his first term in office during his Second Inaugural Address. By 1941, unemployment had dropped to around 9% (down from around 25% in 1932) but most of the socially directed spending of the New Deal was abandoned once World War II started. While war spending continued to stimulate the economy, it no longer was directed toward the sorts of social programs that had fired the imaginations of New Deal era workers and artists.[55]

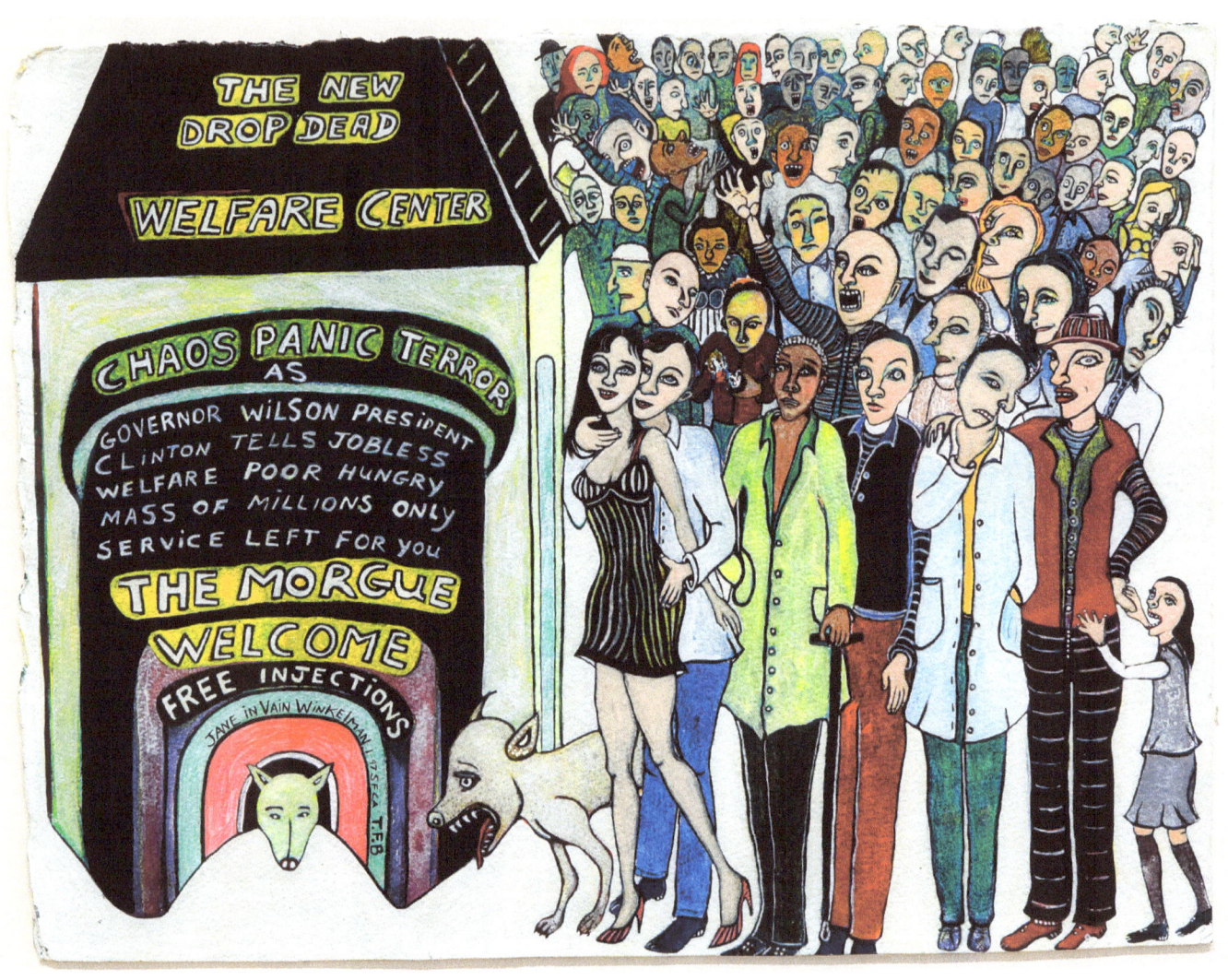

Figure 50.
Jane "in vain" Winkelman
(1949–)
The New Drop Dead Welfare Center, 1997
Painting on Paper, 15 x 20"
Reproduction Courtesy of the Artist

Jane "In Vain" Winkelman experienced homelessness in San Francisco's Tenderloin neighborhood. She was introduced to painting at Hospitality House Community Arts, which provides a safe and supportive space for homeless people to create art. Since 1993, her work has gained wide attention through exhibitions and inclusion in the *Street Sheet*. In this painting Winkelman offers a glimpse of what she felt was the real intention of Clinton era Welfare Reform –to do away with all poor people.

Figure 51.
Richard V. Correll
(1904-1990)
Drought, 1955
Lithograph, 16 x 9"
Reproduction Courtesy of the Estate of
Richard V. Correll

Richard V. Correll was part of a generation of artists who portrayed the strength of those who are suffering rather than their victimization. By portraying their subjects in a noble light, these artists suggested that suffering could also give birth to a new activism against an unjust system. Despite the changing tides of politics and culture, Correll's themes reflected his social conscience throughout his long career. He created countless prints, posters, leaflets, signs, and exhibits for civil rights, Native Americans, senior, labor, environmental and world peace groups. Here, an image from the 1950s looks back at a Dust Bowl farm showing the strength in adversity so often portrayed during the Depression.

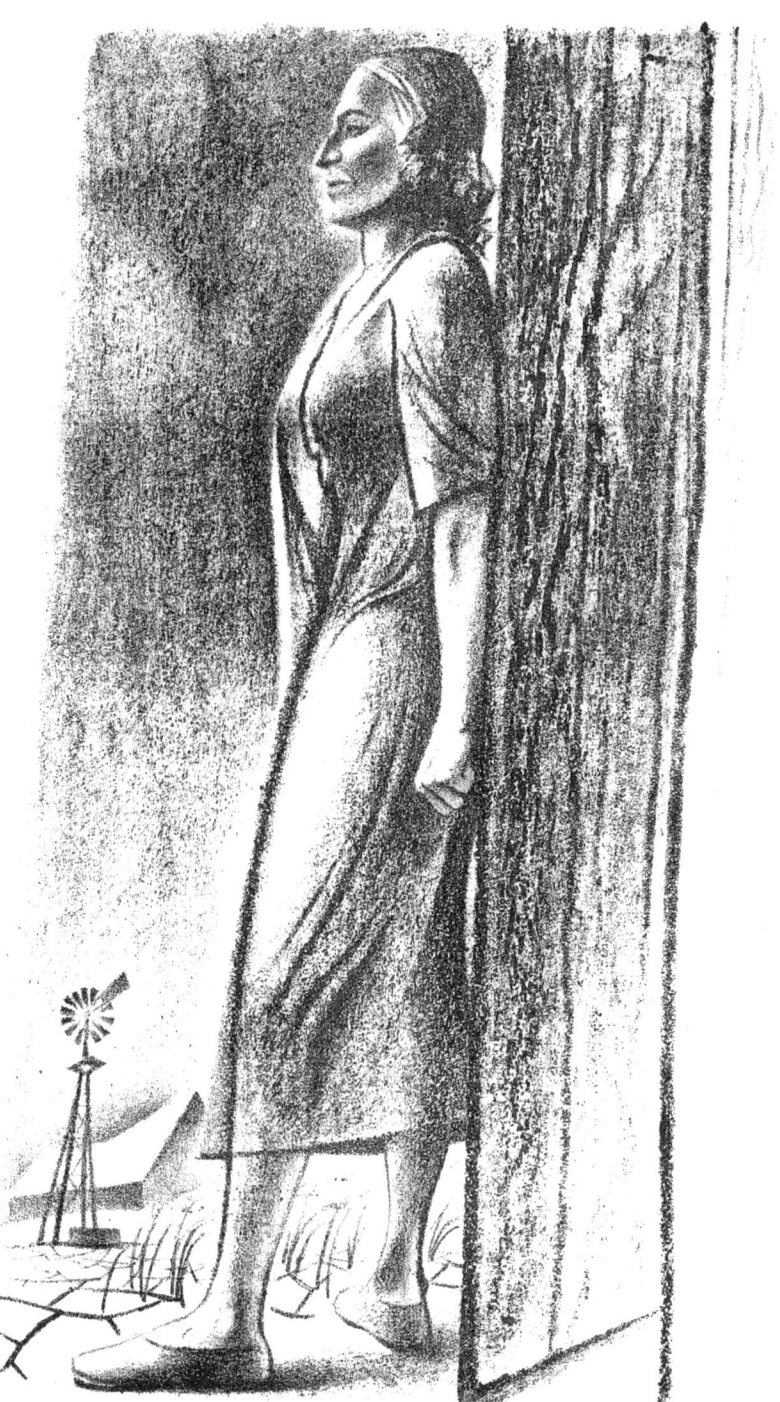

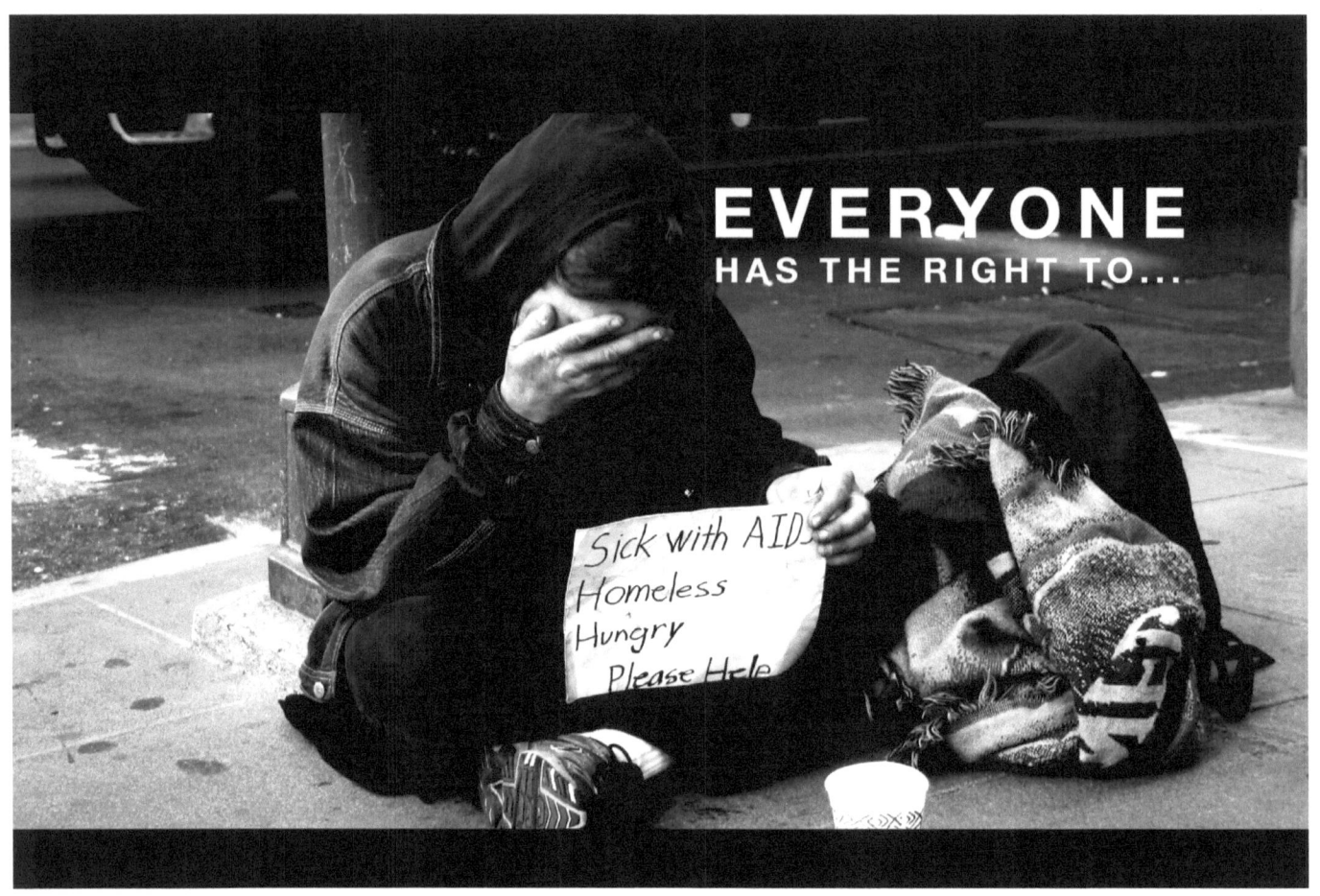

Figure 52.
Robert L. Terrell
(1943-)
Jean McIntosh
(1963-)
Everyone has a right..., 2006
Photocopy, 17 x 22"
Reproduction Courtesy of the Artists

Everyone has a Right, is a series of five photographs of people living on the street in the worst of conditions. Each image is representative of a particularly vulnerable group: the elderly, disabled, ill, children and families. Photocopy posters were created from Robert Terrell's photographs to be put up on the street to draw attention to the failure of the United States to live up to its obligations under the UN's Universal Declaration of Human Rights, recalled by the ironic title of this series.

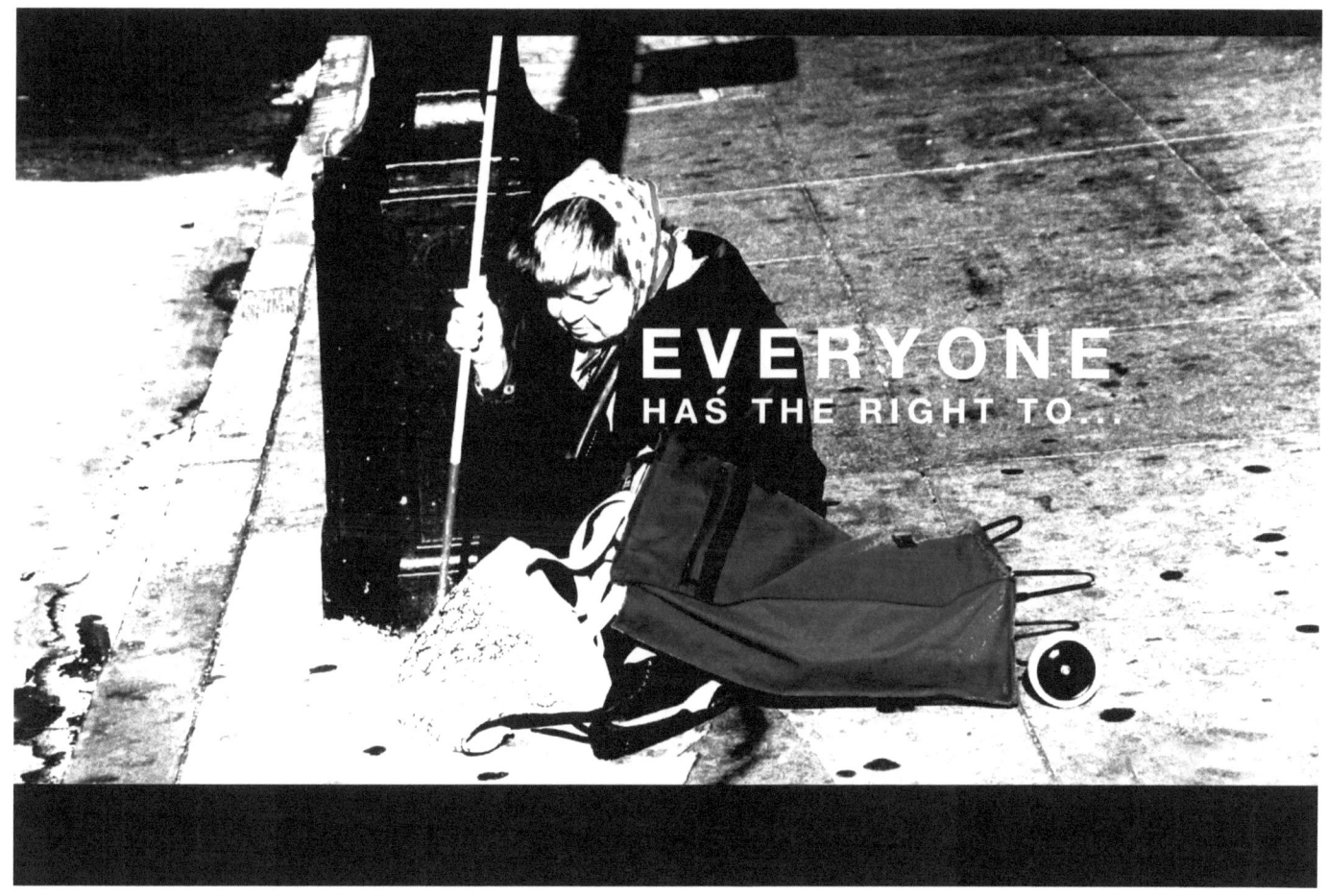

Robert Terrell has spent years photographing and writing about urban poverty all over the world, from Africa and China to the US. His journalism focuses on the global rise in urban poverty as rural work disappears and cities attract more and more people for employment that pays less and less. The brutality of Terrell's imagery is not easy to view. Street photography has a tradition of telling the truth about society, of doubling as its conscience. While exposure to the American Dream turned nightmare is disturbing, there is an implicit assumption that knowledge of such inhuman degradation will spark the viewer's humanity and indignation, prompting action.

Figure 53.
Robert L. Terrell
(1943-)
Jean McIntosh
(1963-)
Everyone has a right..., 2006
Photocopy, 17 x 22"
Reproduction Courtesy of the Artist

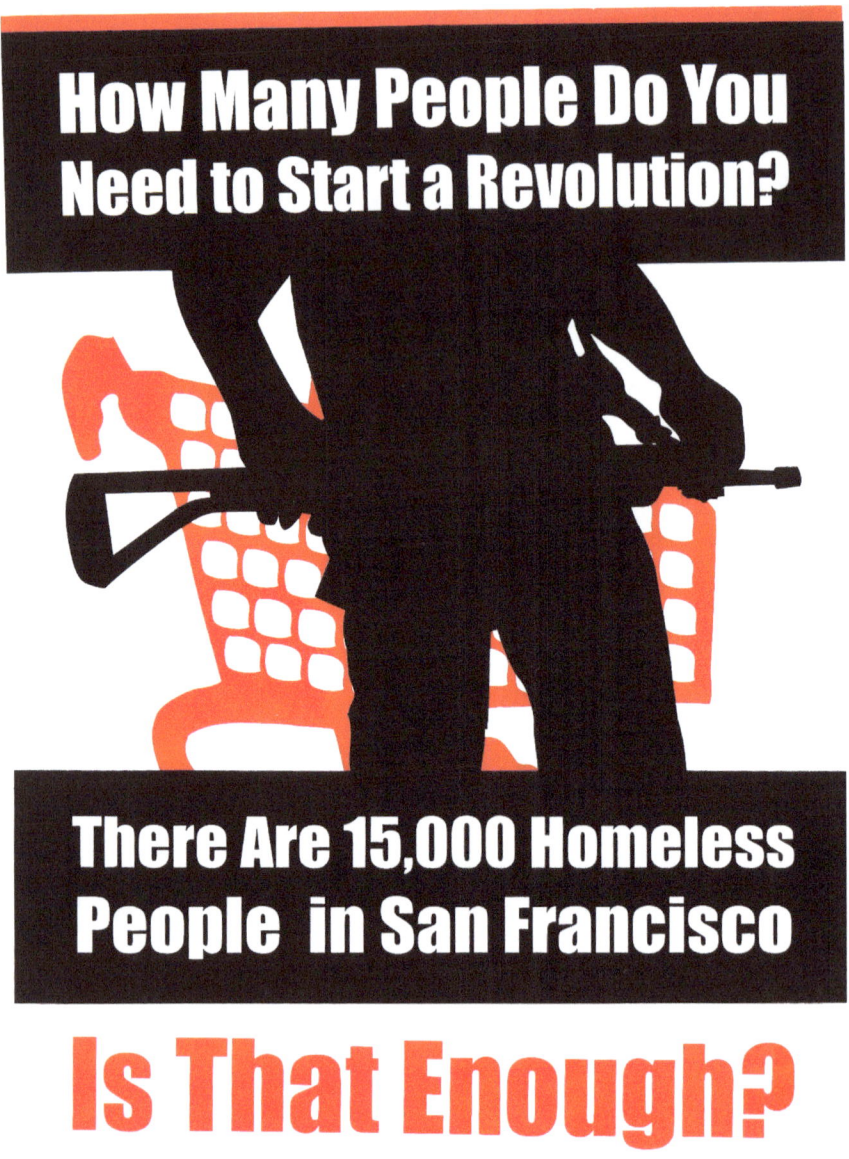

How Many People Do You Need to Start a Revolution?

There Are 15,000 Homeless People in San Francisco

Is That Enough?

sf print collective

Cities across the country have increasingly passed ordinances that criminalize the presence of homeless people rather than attempt to address the root causes of homelessness. Laws against sitting or sleeping in public places, park closures and so-called "public nuisance" laws are all designed to make homelessness disappear. This poster, created as part of a campaign by the San Francisco Print Collective, challenges these attempts to sweep homeless people away. Its militant image offers an angry response to increased criminalization and being pushed further to the margins. It is a call to action to homeless people and their allies to join together and fight back. *How Many People Do You Need to Start a Revolution?* points out the power homeless people have: sheer numbers.

Figure 54.
San Francisco Print Collective, Jesus Barraza
(1978-)
How Many People Do You Need to Start a Revolution?, 2001
Screen Print, 23 x 17 1/2"
Reproduction Courtesy of the Artist

Afterword

Artists and Organizing Today: A Homeless Perspective

Shortly after San Francisco homeless shelters first opened in October of 1982 the mainstream media shifted its presentation of homelessness away from a societal crisis impacting members of our community. Instead it became a portrayal of homeless people as dysfunctional, as coming from outside of San Francisco, and as negatively impacting the good citizens who live here.

By the middle of 1984, then Mayor Dianne Feinstein brought the media on a tour of a South of Market encampment (a latter day Hooverville). She ordered a police sweep and a bulldozer to remove homeless people from the area, thus reintroducing California's "Anti-Okie" approach of violence and police action against people without homes.

The dehumanization of homeless people had begun. They were a health hazard to others. They were dangerous and the police needed to respond to their presence. When the newspaper articles didn't mention urination, defecation, or hypodermic needles in the lead, we knew it was only because it was getting close to Christmas.

A group of us began organizing out of Central City Hospitality House in San Francisco's Tenderloin neighborhood. Hospitality House had been there since the 1960s when it was opened as a community center for kids on the street. It had an art program, and we were surrounded by people making art while we were working together to address the emergency needs of the ever-rising numbers of homeless people. Those days operating out of the art program space at Hospitality House gave birth to our understanding of artwork as an expression of our humanity, anger, hopes and frustration.

By the time we started the Coalition on Homelessness in 1987, our struggle to take control of the portrayal of our own humanity was already at the core of our existence.

In 1989 we created *Street Sheet* to reflect this struggle and it soon became known for the artwork on its pages. Jane "in vain" Winkelman came out of the Hospitality House art program. Joseph De Neri created powerful political cartoons. Tom McCarthy and his comic strips came to us from the local community newspaper, the *Tenderloin Times*. And Eliza Miller set the stage for the graphic look of the paper with her bold woodcut prints. Other artists came on over the years, including Ed Gould, Art Hazelwood, Claude Moller, Jos Sances, and the San Francisco Print Collective. In 1996, the American Friends Service Committee adopted the *Street Sheet* model and established *Street Spirit* in the East Bay with artwork as a vital part of that endeavor.

Some of the Coalition's most effective campaigns have involved artwork in bus shelters and kiosks along Market Street. They have generated wide media attention and public dialogue which would not have occurred with mere writing, speeches or direct actions. It was the use of art that people reacted to and it was the message the artwork was expressing – a message that originated in the Coalition, not simply from the artists themselves. It was art that caused people to stop, think and react.

One campaign called "The Mirror" portrayed comments overheard by *Street Sheet* vendors and reported back to the Coalition, comments so visceral and nasty that they held up a mirror to society and showed people the ugliness of fear and hate. Another campaign contrasted New Deal job programs to contemporary beliefs about homelessness, with the tag line, "Homeless people have been known to build more than huts out of cardboard boxes." The poster showed several WPA buildings built in San Francisco during the New Deal era.

In 2005, when the Coalition, *Street Spirit* and our allies in the East Bay, Portland, Los Angeles and Seattle created Western Regional Advocacy Project (WRAP) to bring our collective voices to the federal government, artwork again played a pivotal role in our organizing. WRAP's first collective project was the release of *Without Housing: Decades of Federal Housing Cutbacks, Massive Homelessness and Policy Failures*. Thanks to a group of artists organized by Art Hazelwood, Without Housing was able to bring life to the words and data (figure #14, 36). Incorporating WRAP's data charts with art to tell the story of the numbers in human terms became the signature aspect of the report and why it is still in demand.

Today, communities across the country are suffering from a criminalization of poverty. The precise laws used in local municipalities differ, be they tickets or arrests for sitting on benches or sleeping in doorways, but their objective is always the same: to remove poor and homeless people from public view. We are united in working with artists in our communities to oppose this growing war on the poor. Art provides a universal message that exposes the brutality of the oppression thrust upon us with discriminatory policing, private security guards in public spaces, gentrification, and modern American "Bum Blockades."

When artists bring their skills and the tools they possess to the community's struggle for social justice, their work shows the strength and humanity that is at the core of every authentic poor people's movement. One powerful image can lay waste to a thousand racist, classist political slogans. Images can move people in their hearts. They give poor people a "mirror" to hold up against false stereotypes and proclaim, "This is who we really are."

Artwork as part of a movement is a vital organizing tool, reaching people who may never listen to a word we say or read an article we write. But it also builds artists as organizers; it deepens their commitment and understanding, and connects them closer to the people whose message needs to be represented. As community organizers need to listen, reflect, and respond to a community, so, too, do artists.

And finally, artwork as part of a movement lets artists as a group become an integral part of their community. They have a role in building a country that respects and values the humanity of us all.

Paul Boden

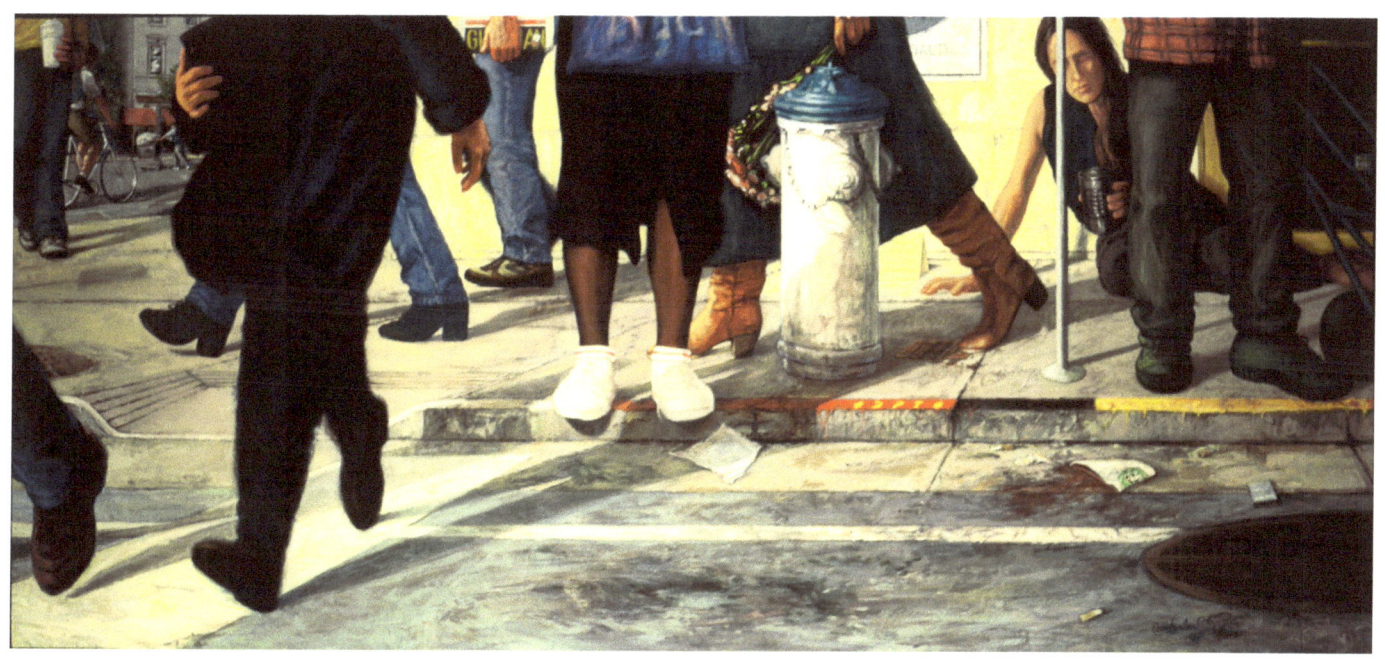

Christine Hanlon uses the principles of the golden section to construct her compositions. The golden section has been used since the Renaissance in the visual arts as a way of using mathematical rules in developing the relation between shapes. In this painting, the golden sections are used by Hanlon to draw attention to the eye level of the homeless person sitting on the sidewalk. Through this carefully planned composition Hanlon brings the viewer into direct relation with the homeless woman, while all around the world passes by in disinterest. It's as if the viewer has taken on the viewpoint of the woman sitting alone in the crowd.

Figure 55.
Christine Hanlon
(1954-)
Faux Street Revisited, 1997
Oil on Canvas, 37 1/2 x 84"
Reproduction Courtesy of the Artist

Notes

1 Bacon, David, *The Children of NAFTA, Labor Wars on the U.S./Mexico Border,* 2004, Berkeley, University of California Press.

2 Some of the Fashion Shows in Bay Area Museums: Fine Arts Museums of San Francisco: de Young Museum, Yves Saint Laurent, November 1, 2008 - April 5, 2009. Fine Arts Museums of San Francisco: Legion of Honor, Artistic Luxury: Fabergé, Tiffany, Lalique, February 7, 2009 - May 31, 2009. Yerba Buena Center for the Arts, Nick Cave: Meet Me at the Center of the Earth, March 28 – July 25, 2009.

3 Hamod, Sam, "Today's Alternative News, Lies About Employment Figures and Living Wages," Sept. 13, 2002. http://www.todaysalternativenews.com/index.php?event=link,150&values[0]=2&values[1]=126

4 *Without Housing: Decades of Federal Housing Cutbacks, Massive Homelessness and Policy Failures,* Western Regional Advocacy Project, San Francisco, Appendix C, note 3.

5 Aid to Families with Dependent Children (AFDC) was established by the Social Security Act of 1935 as a grant program to enable states to provide cash welfare payments for needy children who had been deprived of parental support or care because their father or mother was absent from the home, incapacitated, deceased, or unemployed. AFDC was ended in 1996. http://aspe.hhs.gov/hsp/abbrev/afdc-tanf.htm

6 Press Release, Senate Banking Committee, Senator Phil Gramm, Chairman, 11/12/99, "We are here today to repeal Glass-Steagall because we have learned that government is not the answer." http://banking.senate.gov/prel99/1112gbl.htm

7 Loftis, Anne. 1998. *Witnesses to the Struggle: Imaging the 1930s California Labor Movement,* University of Nevada Press, p.109.

8 Poverty numbers in the Depression http://www.u-s-history.com/pages/h1528.html

9 Kusmer, Kenneth L., *Down and Out, On the Road: The Homeless in American History,* Oxford University Press, 2002, p. 194.

10 DeNavas-Walt, Carmen, Bernadette D. Proctor, and Jessica C. Smith, U.S. Census Bureau, Current Population Reports, P60-238, *Income, Poverty, and Health Insurance Coverage in the United States: 2009,* U.S. Government Printing Office, Washington, DC, 2010. p. 14.

Ganeva, Tana, "47.8 Million People Live in Poverty - Far More Than Previously Thought" Sourced from AlterNet.org, January 5, 2011,

11 *Without Housing: Decades of Federal Housing Cutbacks Massive Homelessness and Policy Failures,* 2010 Update, Western Regional Advocacy Project, San Francisco.

12 Bureau of Labor Statistics National Unemployment rates, August, 2010, http://www.bls.gov/web/laus/laumstrk.htm

California County unemployment rates, 2009 annual averages ftp://ftp.bls.gov/pub/special.requests/la/laucnty09.txt

13 Eckholm, Erik, "Surge Seen in Number of Homeless Veterans," New York Times, November 8, 2007, http://www.nytimes.com/2007/11/08/us/08vets.html

National Coalition for Homeless Veterans, http://www.nchv.org/background.cfm#facts

14 *Without Housing, 2010 Update,* p. 6.

15 *Without Housing, 2010 Update,* p. 8.

16 *Without Housing, 2010 Update,* pp. 33 – 34,

Department of Housing and Urban Development http://www.hudhre.info/HPRP/

17 Kusmer, Kenneth L., p. 202.

18 "The Roosevelt reforms went far beyond previous legislation. They had to meet two pressing needs: to reorganize capitalism in such a way to overcome the crisis and stabilize the system; also, to head off the alarming growth of spontaneous rebellion in the early years of the Roosevelt administration — organization of tenants and the unemployed movements of self-help, general strikes in several cities. … But the New Deal's organization of the economy was aimed mainly at stabilizing the economy, and secondly at giving enough help to the lower classes to keep them from turning a rebellion into a real revolution." Zinn, Howard, *A People's History of the United States,* Harper Perennial, NY, 1980, pp 393-405.

19 Kusmer, Kenneth L., page 208 – 217.

20 Social Security Act of 1935 http://www.ssa.gov/history/35actpre.html

21 Farm Security Administration

http://www.answers.com/topic/farm-security-administration.

22 Platt, Susan, *Art and Politics In the 1930s: Modernism – Marxism – Americanism: A History of Cultural Activism During the Depression Years, 1999,* Midmarch Arts Press, New York.

McCoy, Garnett, "Life of the People," essay in, Life of the People: Realist Prints and Drawings from the Ben and Beatrice Goldstein Collection, 1912-1948, 2000, Library of Congress.

23 Stone, Lee, unpublished lecture on the WPA, 2009.

O'Connor, Francis V., The New Deal Art Projects: An Anthology of Memoirs. Washington, D.C.: Smithsonian Institution Press, 1972, pg. 164. citing memoirs of Jacob Kainen.

24 Platt, Susan, page 179.

Stone, Lee, conversations with Misch Kohn as reported in personal correspondence.

25 Roy Stryker interview http://www.aaa.si.edu/collections/oralhistories/transcripts/stryke63.htm

26 For a general overview of the *New Masses* http://www.spartacus.schoolnet.co.uk/JmassesN.htm

27 Platt, Susan, page 150.

28 Associated American Artists http://en.wikipedia.org/wiki/Associated_American_Artists

29 Skovgaad, John, "The California Labor School," unpublished research article.

30 The TGP's mission statement, as expressed by Olivia Peralta in 1949, sought "to educate and orient the masses, in this way aiding them to liberate themselves." (TGP, Mexico, Hannes Meyer, La Estampa Mexicana, Mexico D.F. 1949).

31 *Roofs for 40 million: an exhibition on housing* - presented by an American Group, inc., With an essay by Lewis Mumford, American Group. Rockefeller Center, New York : American Group, undated.

32 Mexico had a reputation for welcoming political activists on the run and became a natural magnet for international artists, thanks to the former leftist president, Lázaro Cárdenas (1934 - 1940),. Diana Anhalt, *A Gathering of Fugitives,* Archer Books, Santa Maria, CA 2001, p. 36.

33 Rockwell Kent Gallery and Collection of the Plattsburgh State Art Museum, State University of New York, http://clubs.plattsburgh.edu/museum/rk_bio.htm

ACLU discussion of the case Kent vs. Dulles, http://aclu.procon.org/view.resource.php?resourceID=389

34 Two earlier murals, both in 1934, are fitting bookends to the story of the Refregier mural. The Coit Tower murals in San Francisco which were the first mural project of the Roosevelt Administration also faced media and politicians' calls for their destruction. And in New York at Rockefeller Center the mural that Diego Rivera was commissioned to paint was chiseled off the wall by order of owner Nelson Rockefeller when Rivera refused to remove the face of Lenin. Rivera repainted the mural at the Palacio de Bellas Artes in Mexico City. The Coit Tower murals were saved by artists who surrounded the building to prevent their destruction.

35 Correll, Leslie, *Richard V. Correll: Prints and Drawings,* Oakland, Correll Studios, 2005.

36 Fritz Eichenberg, Dorothy Day and the Catholic Worker http://www.gratefulness.org/giftpeople/FritzEichenberg.htm http://www.cjd.org/paper/daprile.html

37 The final Congressional vote on the G.I. Bill was very close, with some opposing because Black veterans would benefit, others opposing because paying veterans $20 a month would "discourage them from working." The fear of a repeat of the Bonus Marchers from twelve years earlier certainly influenced the final outcome. Wilson, Reginald, "G.I. Bill and the transformation of America," The National Forum, Fall 1995. http://findarticles.com/p/articles/mi_qa3651/is_199510/ai_n8720508/

38 "The Fillmore," KQED, Public Broadcasting Service http://www.pbs.org/kqed/fillmore/learning/time.html

39 Caina, Bobby. "Monument to Filipinos' legacy rises in San Francisco, '77 hotel standoff displaced many," Boston Globe, July 7, 2005.

Roberts, Evan, "Remembering the I-Hotel evictions," KALW News, 8/4/2010, http://kalwnews.org/audio/2010/08/04/remembering-i-hotel-evictions_508605.html

40 Reagan and deinstitutionalization as Governor of California - http://pn.psychiatryonline.org/content/38/22/28.1.full as President - http://www.sociology.org/content/vol003.004/thomas.html

41 Connor, Marykate, "The Mass Imprisonment of People with Psychiatric Disabilities In the United States," 8/10/07, unpublished paper, Caduceus Outreach Services.

42 Funk, Maria. and Langone, Carol. "Mental health services innovation and linkage with Los Angeles County Jail" Paper presented at the annual meeting of the American Society of Criminology (ASC), 2009-05-24 http://www.allacademic.com/meta/p126245_index.html

43 *Without Housing, 2010 Update,* p. 16.

44 Clarke, Ben "S.F. Daily Papers Pit Middle Class against Homeless," Media File, Fall 1999 http://www.media-alliance.org/article.php?id=549

45 "The 'dangerous class,' the social scum (lumpenproletariat), that passively rotting mass thrown off by the lowest layers of old society, may, now and then, be swept into the movement by a proletarian revolution; its conditions of life, however, prepare it far more for the part of bribed tool of reactionary intrigue." Marx, Engels, *The Communist Manifesto*, pp. 20-21, Harlan Davidson edition.

46 Mike Rotkin. http://www.mikerotkin.com/

An Open Letter to Mayor Mike Rotkin and Vice-Mayor Ryan Coonerty, August 1, 2010, http://peacecamp2010.blogspot.com/2010/08/open-letter-to-mayor-mike-rotkin-and.html

47 Eleanor Roosevelt http://www.un.org/rights/HRToday/declar.htm

48 Brechin, Gray, "Politics and Modernism: The Trial of the Rincon Annex Murals," in On the Edge of America: California Modernist Art, 1900-1950. edited by Paul Karlstrom, J., pp. 68-93, Berkeley: University of California Press, 1996, p. 69.

49 Housing Assistance Council (2005). Section 515 Rural Rental Housing Program, FY 1963 – FY 2005.

50 Personal correspondence, David Bacon.

51 Steinbeck, John, *The Grapes of Wrath*, 1939.

52 Giczy, Hailey, "The Bum Blockade: Los Angeles and the Great Depression," Voces Novae: Chapman University Historical Review, Vol 1, No 1 (2009).

53 Oklahoma Historical Society's, Encyclopedia of Oklahoma History and Culture, http://digital.library.okstate.edu/encyclopedia/entries/O/OK007.html

54 Pierce, Margo, "Today attacks on homeless people continues to rise nationwide," Street Sheet, July 1-14, 2010, p. 1, Coalition on Homelessness, San Francisco. Additional data for the article from National Coalition for the Homeless.

55 Walker, Richard A., Brechin, Gray, "The Living New Deal: The Unsung Benefits of the New Deal for the United States and California," Working Papers, 08/01/2010 Institute for Research on Labor and Employment University of California, Berkeley http://escholarship.org/uc/item/6c1115sm

A Note on Permissions
Every effort was made to find and contact artists and heirs to obtain permission for the reproduction of works in this book. Unfortunately one proved impossible to locate. Many institutions and individuals would be very happy to know who has the rights to the work of Iver Rose. Freedom Voices looks forward to learning this information and allowing the work to be distributed with proper credit.

List of Artwork

Front cover:
Paul Weller (1912- 2000)
Home, c. 1937
Lithograph, 10 1/2 x 14 1/2"
Reproduction Courtesy of Estate of Paul
Weller
From the Collection of M. Lee Stone Fine
Prints, Inc., San Jose, CA
Photo Credit: Robert Berger Photography

Back cover:
Christine Hanlon (1954-)
Third Street Corridor, 1998
Oil on Canvas, 30 x 52"
Reproduction Courtesy of the Artist

Frontispiece:
Charles Surendorf (1906-1979)
The Jungle, c. 1940
Block Print, 5 x 6"
Courtesy of Surendorf Gallery Collection

Figure 1.
Dorothea Lange (1895-1965)
*Mother and Two Children on The Road Tule-
lake, Siskiyou County, California,* 1939/1975
Library of Congress photograph on Agfa
Portriga paper, 8 x 9 3/4"
Reproduction Courtesy of the Prints and
Photographs Division, Library of Congress,
Washington, D.C.
Collection of de Saisset Museum, Santa
Clara University, NDA.6.686

Figure 2.
David Bacon (1948-)
*San Diego, Indigenous women and children
are part of the community of farm workers
from Oaxaca, living in a camp on a hillside
outside Del Mar, California,* 2005
Photograph, 16 x 24"
Reproduction Courtesy of the Artist

Figure 3.
Bernarda Bryson Shahn (1903 – 2004)
A Mule and a Plow, 1935 – 1937, lithograph
on paper, 43 x 30", Courtesy of the Prints

and Photographs Division, Library of Congress, Washington, D.C.

Figure 4.
Rockwell Kent (1882-1971)
And Now Where?, 1936
Lithograph, 13 x 9 3/8"
Reproduction Courtesy Plattsburgh State
Art Museum, State University of New York,
SUNY, Rockwell Kent Gallery and Collec-
tion. Bequest of Sally Kent Gorton

Figure 5.
Jacob Burck (1907-1982)
The Lord Provides, 1934
Lithograph, 12 x 9 1/16"
Reproduction Courtesy of Conrad and
Joseph Burck
Collection of M. Lee Stone Fine Prints, San
Jose, CA
Photo Credit: Robert Berger Photography

Figure 6.
Giacomo Giuseppe Patri (1898-1978)
White Collar, 1940, 1st Edition Book
Printed from Original Linocut Blocks, 10
3/4 x 8 1/4"
Reproduction Courtesy of Georges Rey
From the Collection of M. Lee Stone Fine
Prints, San Jose, CA

Figure 7, 8, 9.
Giacomo Giuseppe Patri (1898-1978)
Three Linocut Print Pages from the Book,
White Collar, 1938
Linocut Print Page from the Book, White
Collar, 1938, (6 1/2 x 4 1/4") (6 1/8 x 5")
(4 x 3 3/4")
Reproduction Courtesy of Georges Rey
Photo Credit: Robert Berger Photography

Figure 10.
Leon Carlin (dates unknown)
One Third of a Nation, Walnut St. Theatre,
Philadelphia, 1938
Screenprint poster for Federal Theater
Project.
Reproduction Courtesy of the Prints and
Photographs Division, Library of Congress,
Washington, D.C.

Figure 11.
Richard V. Correll (1904-1990)
Dwellings of the Jobless #3, 1939
Linocut, 8 x 10"
Reproduction Courtesy of Estate of Richard
V. Correll

Figure 12.
Fritz Eichenberg (1901-1990)
Christ of the Breadline, 1953
Wood Engraving, 13 3/4 x 9"
Art © Fritz Eichenberg Trust/Licensed by
VAGA, New York, NY
Collection of University of Rhode Island
Library Special Collections

Figure 13.
Rachael Romero (1953-)
San Francisco Poster Brigade
Fight for the International Hotel, 1977,
Offset Poster, 22 1/2 x 17 3/4"
Reproduction Courtesy of the Artist. All
Rights Reserved.
Collection of poster archive of Inkworks
Press, Berkeley, CA

Figure 14.
Art Hazelwood (1961-)
Spirit of Abandon, 2006
Screen Print, 18 x 21"
Reproduction Courtesy of the Artist
Loaned for the exhibition by Western Re-
gional Advocacy Project

Figure 15.
Street Sheet, November 1996,
cover image by **William F. Wolff**, 17 x 11"

Figure 16.
Street Sheet, May 1998,
cover image by **Eliza Miller,** 17 x 11"

Figure 17.
Street Spirit, June 2007,
cover images by **Christine Hanlon** (top),
Tammy Grubbs (bottom), 17 x 11"

Figure 18.
Street Spirit, March 2008,
cover image by **Nili Yosha,** 17 x 11"

Figure 19.
Eric Drooker (1958-)
Under Bridges, The New Yorker,
March 1995, 11 x 8"

Figure 20.
Eric Drooker (1958-)
Under Bridges, 1995
Painting, 11 x 15"
Reproduction Courtesy of the Artist

Figure 21.
San Francisco Print Collective
33% of Homeless are Veterans, 2006
Screen Print, 22 x 16 1/2"
Reproduction Courtesy of the SFPC

Figure 22.
Iver Rose (1899-1972)
Bread Line, 1935
Lithograph, 15 x 17 3/8"
From the Collection of M. Lee Stone Fine
Prints, San Jose, CA
Photo Credit: Robert Berger Photography

Figure 23.
Kiki Smith (1954-)
Home, 2006
Color spit bite aquatint with flat bite, hard
ground and soft ground etching, and dry-
point printed on gampi paper chine collé
26 1/2 x 31" Edition of 20
© Kiki Smith, courtesy The Pace Gallery
Loaned for the exhibition by Crown Point
Press

Figure 24.
Clare Leighton (c 1898-1989)
Bread Line, 1932
Wood Engraving, 12 x 8"
Reproduction with permission from the
estate of Claire Leighton
From the Collection of M. Lee Stone Fine
Prints, San Jose, CA
Photo Credit: Robert Berger Photography

Figure 25.
Christine Hanlon (1954-)
Third Street Corridor, 1998
Oil on Canvas, 30 x 52"
Reproduction Courtesy of the Artist

Figure 26.
Isac Friedlander (1890-1968)
Golddigger, 1932
Wood Engraving, 5 x 3 3/8"
From the Collection of M. Lee Stone Fine
Prints, San Jose, CA
Photo Credit: Robert Berger Photography
Courtesy of the estate of Isac Friedlander

Figure 27.
Eric Drooker (1958-)
Flood! A Novel in Pictures,
Dark Horse Books, paperback
192 pages, 2 color, 9" x 6 1/4"
ISBN# 10: 1-59307-676-2
ISBN# 13: 978-1-59307-676-4
1st Edition ©1992, 2nd Edition ©2002
Special 3rd Edition ©2007

Figure 28, 29.
Jos Sances (1952-)
Holiday Home, 2002
Mixed Media Painting,
Collection of Howard Levine
Reproduction Courtesy of the Artist

Figure 30.
Ed Gould (1932-)
Kindred Spirits, 1997
Woodcut, 8 3/4 x 11 3/4"
Reproduction Courtesy of the Artist

Figure 31.
Albert Potter (1903–1937)
Brother Can You Spare a Dime, 1933/36
Woodcut, 13 x 8"
Reproduction with permission from the
estate of Albert Potter and the Susan Teller
Gallery
From the Collection of M. Lee Stone Fine
Prints, San Jose, CA
Photo Credit: Robert Berger Photography

Page 48.
Lyrics by **E.Y. "Yip" Harburg,**
Music by **Jay Gorney**
Published by Glocca Morra Music (ASCAP)
and Gorney Music (ASCAP)
Administered by Next Decade Entertain-
ment, Inc.
All rights reserved. Used by permission.

Figure 32.
Art Hazelwood (1961-)
Four Freedoms, 1996
Linocut, 14 x 14"
Loaned for the exhibition by the Hearst Art
Gallery, Saint Mary's College of California
Reproduction Courtesy of the Artist

Figure 33.
Herman Volz (1904-1990)
Lockout, c. 1938
Lithograph, 10 3/8 x 15 1/4"
Reproduction with permission from Friedel
Volz. Loaned for the exhibition by M. Lee
Stone Fine Prints, San Jose, CA
Photo Credit: Robert Berger Photography

Figure 34.
Eric Drooker (1958-)
The Hand That Takes, 1997
Digital Print of Original Scratch Board
Drawing, 17 x 11 1/2"
Reproduction Courtesy of the Artist

Figure 35.
Anton Refregier (1905-1979)
San Francisco '34 Waterfront Strike, 1949
Screen Print, 11 1/4 x 22 1/4"
Reproduction with permission from Brigit
Refregier. From the Collection of M. Lee
Stone Fine Prints, San Jose, CA
Photo Credit: Robert Berger Photography

Figure 36.
Claude Moller (1967-)
Housing Crisis, Condition: Critical, 2006
Screen Print, 22 x 16"
Reproduction Courtesy of the Artist
Loaned for the exhibition by Western Re-
gional Advocacy Project

Figure 37.
Doug Minkler (1949-)
Who Drive the Cycle of Poverty? 1997
Screen Print, 20 x 26"
Reproduction Courtesy of the Artist

Figure 38.
Jos Sances (1952-)
Sacred Heart, 2008
Ceramic Tile, 24 x 24"
Reproduction Courtesy of the Artist

Figure 39.
Sandow Birk (1962-)
GI Homecoming, 2008
Oil on Canvas, 30 x 24"
Reproduction Courtesy of the Artist
Loaned for the exhibition by Catharine
Clark Gallery, San Francisco

Figure 40.
Dorothea Lange (1895-1965)
*Scene along "Skid Row," Howard Street, San
Francisco, California,* 1937
Library of Congress photograph on Agfa
Portriga paper, 14 x 11", Reproduction
Courtesy of the Prints and Photographs
Division, Library of Congress, Washington,
D.C. Collection of de Saisset Museum,
Santa Clara University, NDA.6.592

Figure 41.
Dorothea Lange (1895-1965)
*Migrants, family of Mexicans, on road with
tire trouble. Looking for work in the peas.
California.* 1936/1975
Library of Congress photograph on Agfa
Portriga paper, 11 x 14", Reproduction
Courtesy of the Prints and Photographs
Division, Library of Congress, Washington,
D.C. Collection of de Saisset Museum,
Santa Clara University, NDA.6.589
Photo Credit: Robert Berger Photography

Figure 42.
Francisco Dominguez (1959-)
Day Laborer Soup Kitchen, 2008
Silver Gelatin Print, 12 x 18"
Reproduction Courtesy of the Artist

Figure 43.
LIFE Magazine,
June 21, 1937, 14 x 10 1/2"

Figure 44.
Francisco Dominguez (1959-)
*Colusa County, Migrant workers taking a
break from picking squash,* 2003
Silver Gelatin Print, 14 x 14"
Reproduction Courtesy of the Artist

Figure 45.
David Bacon (1948-)
*San Diego, A young Mixtec man with the gui-
tar he brought with him from Oaxaca, playing
the music of his home village,* 2005
Photograph, 16 x 24"
Reproduction Courtesy of the Artist

Figure 46.
Paul Weller (1912-2000)
Harvest Hands, 1937
Lithograph, 11 1/2 x 14 1/2"
Reproduction Courtesy of Estate of Paul
Weller
From the Collection of M. Lee Stone Fine
Prints, Inc., San Jose, CA
Photo Credit: Robert Berger Photography

Figure 47.
Paul Weller (1912-2000)
Home, c. 1937
Lithograph, 10 1/2 x 14 1/2"
Reproduction Courtesy of Estate of Paul
Weller
From the Collection of M. Lee Stone Fine
Prints, Inc., San Jose, CA
Photo Credit: Robert Berger Photography

Figure 48.
Charles Surendorf (1906-1979)
California, 1938
Wood Engraving, 6 x 8"
Courtesy of Surendorf Gallery Collection

Figure 50.
Dorothea Lange (1895-1965)
*The windshield of a migratory agricultural
laborer's car, in a squatter camp near Sacra-*

mento, California, 1936
Library of Congress photograph on Agfa
Portriga paper, 11 x 14". Reproduction
Courtesy of the Prints and Photographs
Division, Library of Congress, Washington,
D.C. Collection of de Saisset Museum,
Santa Clara University, NDA.6.594
Photo Credit: Robert Berger Photography

Figure 51.
Jane "in Vain" Winkelman (1949-)
The New Drop Dead Welfare Center, 1997
Painting on Paper, 15 x 20"
Reproduction Courtesy of the Artist

Figure 50.
Richard V. Correll (1904-1990)
Drought, 1955
Lithograph, 16 x 9"
Reproduction Courtesy of Estate of Richard
V. Correll

Figure 51.
Robert L. Terrell (1943-) and
Jean McIntosh (1963-)
Everyone has a right..., 2006
Photocopy, 17 x 22"
Reproduction Courtesy of the Artists

Figure 52.
Robert L. Terrell (1943-) and
Jean McIntosh (1963-)
Everyone has a right..., 2006
Photocopy, 17 x 22"
Reproduction Courtesy of the Artists

Figure 54.
**San Francisco Print Collective,
Jesus Barraza** (1978-)
*How Many People Do You Need to Start a
Revolution?,* 2001
Screen Print, 23 x 17 1/2"
Reproduction Courtesy of the Artist

Figure 55.
Christine Hanlon (1954 -)
Faux Street Revisited, 1997
Oil on Canvas, 37 1/2 x 84"
Reproduction Courtesy of the Artist

www.ingramcontent.com/pod-product-compliance
Lightning Source LLC
Chambersburg PA
CBHW050853180526

45159CB00007B/2660